Contents

Introduction

This book is about bloody ballads, that is narrative poems with themes as grim and gruesome as a modern-day slasher movie. This may seem strange to those who like their poetry refined and highbrow but, as well as being filled with gripping stories, the Scottish ballads are also written in a lively, rhythmic and very atmospheric style. Much of the poetry written at the same time as the ballads were being collected seems very verbose and flimsy in comparison. After all who really cares about Grecian urns, dancing daffodils and burning tigers when there is rank poison, blood red wine and hat pins used to murder.

Where do the ballads come from? From word of mouth. These ballads circulated around Scotland, England and similar poems are found in many other parts of Europe. They were the entertainment of the day, set to music and sung, listened to and appreciated by an audience of lords, lairds, burgesses and ordinary folk, an audience from all parts of the society of the day.

The themes are mostly dark and grisly: love, sex and death, betrayal and murder, poisoning and drowning and plague, the burning of a pregnant sister by her jealous brother, incest and infanticide, suicide and execution, the slaying of a father by his son because of false advice from a mother – and loss and sorrow, much loss and sorrow. All of the ballads in this book have an unhappy ending, barring two – and only one does not involve the death of one of the main participants.

The ballads are in written in the Scots tongue, most of which is still in use, especially the pronunciation of words. There is a full glossary at the end of the book with some notes, although often speaking the words out loud makes understanding easy. The ballads are very rhythmic and, although narrative, are often sparse in the description of events but detailed in the emotions they evoke, leaving the reader to fill in the gaps and to sympathise with the protagonists. So much would be lost by translating the ballads into modern English but I have standardised spelling and usage.

No doubt there were hundreds of these ballads during the early modern period in Scotland, and it should be said that there would also have been many different versions, according to the taste of the singer and the dialect of the part of the country. It is not certain when they were actually composed because they were not written down until the time of Sir Walter Scott and James Hogg, the Ettrick Shepherd, at which time their popularity was waning because of the spread of the written word. The ballads were still important, though, and much influenced Robert Burns. Sadly, since then, many ballads have undoubtedly been lost, although many of the best survive.

Some of the ballads were gathered together (and 'improved' in some cases, which is not always to a modern reader's taste) in Scott's work *Minstrelsy of the Scottish Border*, first published in 1802. It was, however, Francis James Child, an American scholar and Professor at Harvard University, who made the first comprehensive collection of ballads, *The English and Scottish Popular Ballads*, published between 1882 and 1898. Child regarded the ballads as being more democratic and accessible than most contemporary poetry, as they had been sung and listened to by ordinary folk as well as lords and lairds.

Why are they so violent? Scotland was a violent place and they reflect the times from when they came although, no doubt, they were also composed to grip the listener – and people have always enjoyed the grimmer aspects of life.

As will be seen, the ballads are about lords and ladies and their machinations; none in this collection are primarily about the 'lower orders'. Girls play a larger role than might have been expected in a male-dominated age, although the heroines are usually fair of face, white of skin, yellow of hair and thin of waist (suggesting, of course, they were chaste). Not that, by any means, females are weak or foolish or unwilling participants in the events that overtake them.

In this book are twenty-one of the best bloody ballads, although in a selection of this kind many were omitted that warrant attention. My favourite remains the first, 'The Twa Corbies', which I read in my late teens and has stuck with me through the rest of my life, although (so far) my wife has not taken another mate and no crow feasting on my flesh would consider the dinner sweet…

Charles Sinclair
May 2011

The Twa Corbies

As I was walking all alane,
I heard twa corbies mak a mane;
The tane untae the tither did say,
'Whaur sall we gang and dine the day?'

'In behint yon auld fail dyke,
I wot there lies a new-slain knight,
And naebody kens that he lies there,
But his hawk, his hound, and his lady fair.

'His hound is tae the hunting gane;
His hawk tae fetch the wild fowl hame;
His wife has ta'en another mate;
So we may mak oor dinner sweet.

'Ye'll sit on his white hause-bane,
And I'll pike out his bonny blue een;
Wi' ae lock o' his gowden hair,
We'll theek oor nest when it grows bare.

'Mony an ane for him maks mane,
But none sall ken whaur he is gane;
Owre his white banes, when they are bare,
The wind sall blaw for evermair.'

corbie *crow*   mak a mane *moaning together*   yon *that*
wot *know, have knowledge of*   fail dyke *turf wall*
kens *knows*   mate is pronounced 'meet'   hause-bane *collar bone*
een *eyes*   theek *thatch*   maks mane *laments, bemoans*

1

The Twa Corbies

Two crows are heard talking, discussing where they will find their next meal. One knows of a newly killed knight, whose body remains undiscovered, having been abandoned by his hawk, his hound and his lady fair – the latter having already found a new love. The crows are then at liberty to feast on the corpse, even using the knight's golden hair, usually a token of everlasting love, to line their nest. Although people may mourn the knight, nobody will ever know where he lies and he will rot away in unconsecrated ground until only bones remain.

The implication is that it was the knight's 'lady fair' who slew him, as she is the only person who knows where his body lies; furthermore he has also been spurned by both his hawk and his hound – usually the truest of creatures. This is not only a comment on the vagaries of fortune and true love but on mortality itself: as an old Scottish proverb puts it, 'The king gangs doun, the world gangs round.' In other words, the dead are soon forgotten…

'The Twa Corbies' is in stark contrast to the many of the 'loyalties' of the time, where true and devoted love sees through, even if it is only in death (such as in this book 'Lord William and Fair Annet' and 'The Border Widow's Lament'), including from 'The Thrie Ravens':

> 'O doun intae yon green grass field
> Thaur lies a squire, baith killed and deid;
>
> His horse is standing by his side,
> And thought he should get on and ride;
>
> His hounds were standing by his feet,
> And lick'd his sairs: they were sae deep;
>
> There cam a lady fu' o' wae,
> As big wi' child as she could gae;
>
> She stetch'd hersel doun by his side,
> And for the love o' him she died.'
>
> He was buried in St Mary's kirk,
> And she was buried in St Mary's quire;
>
> Out o' his grave thaur grew a fir,
> And out o' her a lily fair;
>
> They grew till they grew tae the kirk top,
> And thaur they cast a true love knot;
>
> O dinna ye think their love was true,
> When out of their graves sic flowers grew.

'The Twa Corbies' is from Child 29.

Lamkin

It's Lamkin was a mason good,
　　As ever built wi' stane;
He built Lord Wearie's castle,
　　But payment got he nane.

'O pay me, Lord Wearie,
Come, pay me my fee.'—
'I canna pay you, Lamkin,
For I maun gang owre the sea.'

'O pay me now, Lord Wearie,
Come, pay me out o' hand.'—
'I canna pay you, Lamkin,
　　Unless I sell my land.'

'O gin ye winna pay me,
　　I here sall mak a vow,
Before that ye cam hame again,
　　Ye sall hae cause tae rue.'

Lord Wearie got a bonny ship,
　　Tae sail the saut sea faem;
Bade his lady weel the castle keep,
　　Aye till he should cam hame.

But the nurse was a fause limmer
　　As e'er hung on a tree;
She laid a plot wi' Lamkin,
When her lord was owre the sea.

maun *must*　out o' hand *immediately*　gin *if*
saut *salt*　limmer *wretch*　tree *gallows (tree)*

3

Lamkin

She laid a plot wi' Lamkin,
When the servants were awa',
Let him in at a little shot-window,
And brought him tae the ha'.

'O whaur's a' the men o' this hoose,
That ca' me Lamkin?'—
'They're at the barn-well thrashing;
Twill be lang ere they come in.'

'And whaur's the women o' this hoose,
That ca' me Lamkin?'—
'They're at the far well washing;
Twill be lang ere they come in.'

'And whaur's the bairns o' this hoose,
That ca' me Lamkin?'—
'They're at the school reading;
Twill be the night ere they come home.'

'O whaur's the lady o' this hoose,
That ca's me Lamkin?'—
'She's up in her bower sewing,
But we soon can bring her doun.'

Then Lamkin's ta'en sharp knife,
That hang doun by his gaire,
And he hae gien the bonny babe
A deep wound and a' sair.

Then Lamkin he rock'd,
And the fause nurse sang,
Till frae ilkae bore o' the cradle
The red blude out sprang.

shot-window *hinged window* gaire *part of a garment by the knee*
ilka bore *every hole*

4

Lamkin

Then out it spak the lady,
As she stood on the stair;
'What ails my bairn, nurse,
That he's greeting sae sair?

'O still my bairn, nurse,
O still him wi' the pap!'—
'He winna still, lady,
For this nor for that.'

'O still my bairn, nurse,
O still him wi' the wand!'—
'He winna still, lady,
For a' his father's land.'

'O still my bairn, nurse,
O still him wi' the bell!'—
'He winna still, lady,
Till ye cam doun yoursel.'

O the firsten step she steppit,
She steppit on a stane;
But the neisten step she steppit,
She met him Lamkin.

'O mercy, mercy, Lamkin,
Hae mercy upon me!
Though you've ta'en my young son's life,
Ye may let mysel be.'

'O sall I kill her, nurse,
Or sall I let her be?'—
'O kill her, kill her, Lamkin,
For she ne'er was guid tae me.'

pap *breast* wand *rattle, stick* neisten *next*

Lamkin

'O scour the basin, nurse,
  And mak it fair and clean,
For tae keep this lady's heart's blude,
  For she's cam o' noble kin.'

'Thaur need nae basin, Lamkin,
  Let it run through the floor;
What better is the heart's blood
  O the rich than o' the poor?'

But ere three months were at an end,
  Lord Wearie cam again;
But dowie, dowie was his heart
  When first he cam hame.

'O whase blood is this,' he says,
  'That lies in the chamer?'—
'It's your lady's heart's blood;
  Tis as clear as the lamer.'

'And whase blood is this,' he says,
  'That lies in my ha'?'—
'It is your young son's heart's blood;
  Tis the clearest o' a'.'

O sweetly sang the black bird
  That sat upon the tree;
But sairer greet Lamkin,
  When he was condemn'd tae die.

And bonny sang the mavis,
  Out on the thorny brake;
But sairer greet the nurse,
  When she was tied tae the stake.

dowie *doleful, sorrowing* chamer *chamber* lamer *amber*
mavis *thrush* brake *thicket*

6

Lamkin

Notes

Lamkin is a builder who builds Lord Wearie a fine castle, but Lord Wearie refuses him his fee, saying that he could only afford it if he sold his land. Lamkin curses him. Aided by the wicked wet-nurse, Lamkin manages to enter the castle when the servants are all away. The two conspirators lure the lady of the house from her bower by stabbing her infant child in his cot so cruelly that it screams. The wailing alerts the lady, who comes down to tend to the child. Seeing that her baby is dead, the lady pleads for mercy. Lamkin asks the nurse if they should spare her, but the nurse says no and the lady is also savagely murdered. Some months later Lord Wearie returns to find that his lady and son have been slain and he has Lamkin and the nurse executed.

This is one of the cruellest of ballads. Lamkin has certainly been wronged by not being paid, but the revenge Lamkin takes is in innocent life. The crime is even more heinous in that he is aided by the wet-nurse, who not only lets Lamkin breach the castle but then urges him to murder. Lamkin even suggests draining the lady's blood into a basin, redolent of sacramental blood (or making black pudding), until the nurse tells him that rich or poor what is the difference and her blood can drain through the hall floor. That neither Lamkin nor the nurse escape, nor can ever have had a realistic chance of doing so, and are both executed makes their crime even more horrific, being a self-destructive act of vengeance.

It has been suggested that in earlier versions of this ballad Lamkin is actually the Devil and Lord Balwearie breaks his pact to pay Satan, hence the terrible and bloody revenge.

The castle in question is suggested to be Balwearie Castle, which is a couple of miles south and west of Kirkcaldy in Fife. The castle was built during the time it was held by the Stewarts of Balwearie but now is a shattered ruin.

The ballad is from Child No 93.

The ruin of Balwearie Castle.

Lady Maisry

The young lords o' the north countrie,
Hae a' a wooing gane,
Tae win the love o' Lady Maisry,
But o' them she wad hae nane.

O they hae court'd Lady Maisry
Wi' a' kin kind o' things;
And they hae sought her, Lady Maisry,
Wi' brooches and wi' rings.

And they hae sought her, Lady Maisry,
Frae father and frae mother;
And they hae sought her, Lady Maisry,
Frae sister and frae brother.

And they hae follow'd her, Lady Maisry,
Through chamber and through ha';
But a' that they could say tae her,
Her answer still was 'na'.

'O haud your tongues, young men,' she says,
'And think nae mair o' me;
For I've gien my love to ain English lord,
And think nae mair o' me.'

Her father's kitchy-boy heard that,
And ill death may he die!
And he is on tae her brother,
As fast as gang could he.

a' kin *every*

Lady Maisry

'O is my father and my mother weel,
　　But and my brothers three?
Gin my sister Lady Maisry's weel,
　　There's naething can ail me.'

'Your father and your mother's weel,
　　But and your brothers three;
Your sister Lady Maisry's weel,
　　So big wi' bairn gangs she.'

'Gin this be true ye tell tae me,
　　My malison light on thee!
But gin it be a lie you tell,
　　You sall be hangit hie.'

He's done him tae his sister's bower,
　　Wi' meikle dule and care;
And there he saw her Lady Maisry,
　　Kaiming her yellow hair.

'O wha is aught that bairn,' he says,
　　'That ye sae big are wi'?
And gin ye winna own the truth,
　　This moment ye sall die!'

She turn'd her right and round about,
　　And the kaim fell frae her hand;
A trembling seiz'd her fair body,
　　And her rosy cheek grew wan.

'O pardon me, my brother dear,
　　And the truth I'll tell to thee;
My bairn it is tae Lord William,
　　And he is betroth'd tae me.'

but and *and also*　gin *if*　bairn *child*　malison *curse*　meikle *much*
dule *grief*　kaiming *combing*　wha is aught *whose*

Lady Maisry

'O could nae ye hae gotten dukes or lords,
  Intill yer ain countrie,
That ye draw up wi' an English dog,
  Tae bring this shame on me?

'But ye maun gie up the English lord,
  When your young babe is born;
For, gin you keep him an hour langer,
  Your life sall be forlorn.'

'I will gie up this English blude,
  Till my young babe be born;
But the ne'er a day nor hour langer,
  Though my life should be forlorn.'

'O whaur is a' my merry young men,
  Whom I gie meat and fee,
Tae pu' the thistle and the thorn,
  Tae burn this vile whore wi'?'

'O whaur will I gie a bonny boy,
  Tae help me in my need,
Tae rin wi' haste tae Lord William,
  And bid him come wi' speed?'

O out and spake a bonny boy,
  Stood by her brother's side:
'Or I would run your errand, lady,
  Owre a' the world wide.

'Aft I hae run your errands, lady,
  When blawn baith win and weet;
But now I'll run your errand, lady,
  Wi' sat tears on my cheek.'

draw up *take up* maun *must* forlorn *lost*
fee *money* rin *run*

10

Lady Maisry

O when he cam tae broken briggs,
He bent his bow and swam,
And when he cam tae the green grass growing,
He slack'd his shoon and ran.

O when he cam tae Lord William's gates,
He ba'ed nae tae chap or ca',
But set his bent bow to his breast,
And lightly lap the wa';
And, or the porter was at the gate,
The boy was in the ha'.

'O is my biggins broken, boy?
Or is my towers won?
Or is my lady lighter yet,
O' a dear daughter or a son?'

'Your biggin is nae broken, sir,
Nor is your towers won;
But the fairest lady in a' the land,
For ye this day maun burn.'

'O saddle me the black, black steed,
Or saddle me the broun;
O saddle me the swiftest steed,
That ere rode frae a toun.'

Or he was near a mile awa',
She heard his wild horse sneeze:
'Mend up the fire, my false brother,
It's nae cam tae my knees.'

briggs *bridges*   shoon *shoes*   ba'ed *waited*   chap *knock*
lap *leapt*   or *before*   biggins *buildings*

Lady Maisry

O when he lighted at the gate,
She heard his bridle ring:
'Mend up the fire, my false brother,
It's far yet frae my chin.

'Mend up the fire tae me, brother,
Mend up the fire tae me;
For I see him coming hard and fast,
Will soon mend it up tae thee.

'O gin my hands hae been loose, Willy,
Sae hard as they are bound,
I would hae turn'd me frae the gleed,
And casting out your young son.'

'O I'll gar burn for you, Maisry,
Your father and your mother;
And I'll gar burn for you, Maisry,
Your sister and your brother.

'And I'll gar burn for you, Maisry,
The chief o' a' your kin;
And the last bonfire that I come tae,
Mysel I will cast in.'

lighted *got down*   gleed *fire*   gar *cause to happen*

Lady Maisry

NOTES

Lady Maisry is courted by many lords and noblemen but she is not interested in any of them, despite their great persistence. To get rid of them, she tells then that she is in love with an English lord, Lord William. A kitchen boy runs off to tell Maisry's brother, informing him that, not only is Maisry in love with an English man, she is also heavy with his child. Her brother is furious: he is dishonoured by his sister's behaviour (seemingly far more upset that the father of the child is an Englishman than because his sister is actually pregnant – at least in this version), and seeks out Maisry in her bower, threatening to kill her if she does not abandon her lover. This she refuses to do, so her brother gets his men to gather to fuel and decides to burn his heavily pregnant sister, presumably supported by the rest of her family. A fellow hurries off to tell Lord William, and he takes his swiftest horse and rides to save Maisry. But poor Maisry is already being torched and, although they pass a few words, she cannot be saved. Lord William promises that he will burn the rest of her family, before finally casting himself into the flames.

Lady Maisry is so devoted to Lord William that not only is she willing to be burnt rather than lose him, she also provokes her brother by goading him that he has not killed her yet, even as the flames are coming higher about her.

The ballad is from Child No 65 and, like most of the ballads, there are many different versions.

Lord Thomas and Fair Annet

Lord Thomas and Fair Annet
Sat a' day on a hill;
When night was come and the sun was set,
They hadna talk'd their fill.

Lord Thomas said a word in jest,
(Fair Annet took it ill),
'A, I will never wed a wife
Against my ain friends' will.'

'If ye will ne'er wed a wife,
A wife will ne'er wed ye!'
Sae he is hame tae tell his mither,
And knelt upon his knee.

'O rede, O rede, mither,' he says,
'A good rede gie tae me:
O sall I tak the nut-brown bride,
And let Fair Annet be?'

'The nut-brown bride has gowd and gear,
Fair Annet she's gat nane;
And the little beauty Fair Annet haes,
O it will soon by gane.'

And he has tae his brother gane:
'Now, brother, rede ye me;
A, sall I marry the nut-brown bride,
And cast Fair Annet bye.'

friends *relatives*   rede *advice, advise*
a guid rede gie tae me *give me a good piece of advice*   gear *property*

Lord Thomas and Fair Annet

'The nut-brown bride has oxen, brother,
The nut brown bride has kye;
I wad hae ye marry the nut-brown bride,
And cast Fair Annet bye.'

'Her oxen may die in the house, billie,
And her kye intae the byre,
And I sall hae nothing tae mysell
But a fat fadge by the fire.'

And he has tae his sister gane:
'Now, sister, rede ye me;
O sall I marry the nut-brown bride,
And set Fair Annet free?'

'I'se rede ye tak Fair Annet, Thomas,
And let the brown bride alane;
Let ye should sigh, and say, 'Alace,
What is this we brought hame?'

'No, I will tak my mother's counsel,
And marry me out o' hand;
And I will tak the nut-brown bride,
Fair Annet may leave the land.'

Up then rose Fair Annet's father,
Twa hours or it were day,
And he is gane intae the bower
Wherein Fair Annet lay.

'Rise up, rise up, Fair Annet,' he says,
'Put on your silken sheene;
Let us gae tae St Mary's kirk,
And see the rich weddeen.'

kye *cattle* billie *brother* byre *cow-house*
fadge *round thick loaf (dumpy person)* or *before* alace *alas* weddeen *wedding*

15

Lord Thomas and Fair Annet

'My maids, gae tae my dressing room,
And dress tae me my hair;
Whaur e'er ye laid a plait before,
See ye lay ten times mair.

'My maid, gae tae my dressing room,
And dress tae me my smock;
The ane half is o' the holland fine,
The other o' the needle-work.'

The horse Fair Annet rode upon,
He amblit like the wind;
Wi' siller he was shod before,
Wi' burning gowd behind.

Four and twenty siller bells
Were a' tied tae his mane,
And yae tift o' the Norland wind,
They tinkl'd ane by ane.

Four and twenty gay guid knights
Rode by Fair Annet's side,
And four and twenty ladies,
As gin she hae been a bride.

And when she cam to Mary's kirk,
She sat on Mary's stane:
The cleading that Fair Annet hae,
It skinkl'd in their een.

And when she cam intae the kirk,
She shimmer'd like the sun;
The belt that was about her waist
Was a' wi' pearls bedone.

holland *linen* amblit *rode* siller *silver* yae tift *any breeze* norland *north*
weddeen *wedding* gin *if* cleading *clothing* skinkl'd *sparkled* bedone *decorated*

Lord Thomas and Fair Annet

She sat her by the nut-brown bride,
And her e'en they were sae clear,
Lord Thomas, he clean forgot the bride,
When Fair Annet drew near.

He had a rose in his hand,
He gae it kisses three,
And reaching by the nut-brown bride,
Laid in on Fair Annet's knee.

Up then spake the nut-brown bride,
She spake wi' meikle spite:
'And whaur gat ye that rose-water,
That does mak ye sae white?'

'O I did gae the rose-water
Whaur ye will ne'er gae nane,
For I did gae that very rose-water
Intae my mother's wame.'

The bride she drew a long bodkin
Frae out her gay head-gear,
And strake Fair Annet untae the heart,
That word spake never mair.

Lord Thomas he saw Fair Annet wax pale,
And marvelit what might be;
But when he saw her dear heart's blood,
A' wuid wroth wax'd he.

He drew his dagger, that was sae sharp,
That was sae sharp and meet,
And drove it intae the nut-brown bride,
That fell deid at his feet.

meikle *a large amount*   wame *womb*   bodkin *long pin*   marvelit *shocked, amazed*
wax *grow*   wuid wrath *mad with rage*   meet *well-fitting*

Lord Thomas and Fair Annet

'Now stay for me, dear Annet,' he said,
'Now stay, my dear,' he cry'd;
Then strake the dagger untae his heart,
And fell deid by her side.

Lord Thomas was buried without kirk wa',
Fair Annet within the quire,
And o' the tane there grew a birk,
The other a bonny briar.

And ay they grew, and ay they threw,
As they wad fain be near;
And by this ye may ken right weel
That they were twa lovers dear.

quire *choir* birk *birch* threw *intertwined* fain *desirous, eager*

Lord Thomas and Fair Annet

NOTES

Lord Thomas and Fair Annet fall in love but, although a comely girl, Fair Annet is not particularly wealthy. Lord Thomas decides to consult his family about whether he should marry Fair Annet or the nut-brown bride; the latter is plain in looks but has much gold and cattle. Lord Thomas ask his mother and his brother for advice, and they say he should marry wealth rather than beauty, while his sister disagrees and even he realises that when her dowry is spent he will be married to a 'fat fadge'. Abandoning love for wealth, Lord Thomas decides to marry the nut-brown bride anyway.

Fair Annet's father urges her to go to the wedding and, beautifully dressed and coiffed (despite her apparent poverty), Fair Annet grabs the attention of Lord Thomas, who only has eyes for her. The nut-brown bride is not happy and, taking a long pin holding up her hair, stabs Fair Annet through the heart. In a furious rage, Lord Thomas first slays the nut-brown bride in revenge and then kills himself. As she was murdered, the Fair Annet is buried within the church but, as Lord Thomas has committed suicide, his grave is outside the graveyard in unconsecrated ground. Nevertheless from his grave a fir tree grows and from her grave a wild rose and these intertwine and the lovers are finally united in death.

Several motifs are found in this ballad which reappear elsewhere. One is the use of 'four and twenty', which may come from Revelation in *The Bible,* representing the complete Church: the twelve tribes of Israel with the twelve Apostles of the Lamb. Another is the use of 'milk white' to describe the hue of skin, to represent innate virtue, while the nut-brown bride is tainted by more than her skin colour.

The ballad is from Child No 73.

Sir Patrick Spens

The kings sits in Dunfermline toun,
Drinking the blude-red wine:
'O whaur will I get a skeely skipper,
To sail this new ship o' mine?'

O up and sat an eldern knight,
Sat at the king's right knee,
'Sir Patrick Spens is the best sailor,
That e'er sail'd the sea.'

Oor king has written a braid letter,
And seal'd it wi' his hand,
And sent it tae Sir Patrick Spens,
Was walking on the strand.

'To Noroway, to Noroway,
To Noroway oe'r the faem;
The king's daughter of Noroway,
Tis thou maun bring her hame.'

The first word that Sir Patrick read,
Sae loud, loud laugh'd he;
The next word that Sir Patrick read,
The tear blind'd his ee.

'O wha is this hae done this deed,
And told the king o' me,
To send us out at this time o' year,
Tae sail upon the sea?

skeely *skilful*   eldern *old*   maun *must*

20

Sir Patrick Spens

'Be it wind, be it wet, be it hail, be it sleet,
 Oor ship must sail the faem;
The king's daughter of Noroway,
 Tis we maun fetch her hame.'

They hoys'd their sails on a Monday morn,
 Wi' a' the speed they may;
They hae landed in Noroway,
 Upon a Wednesday.

They hadna been a week, a week,
 In Noroway, but tae,
When that the lords o' Noroway
 Began a loud to say:

'Ye Scottishmen spend a' our king's gowd,
 And a' our queenis fee.'—
 'Ye lie, ye lie, ye liars loud!
 Full loud I hear you lie!

'For I brought as much white monie,
 As gane my men and me,
And I brought a half-fou of guid red gowd,
 Out oe'r the sea wi' me.

'Make ready, make ready, my merrymen a'!
 Our guid ship sails the morn.'—
 'Now ever alake, my master dear,
 I fear a deadly storm!

'I saw the new moon, late yestreen,
 Wi' the auld moon in her arm;
And, if we gang to sea, master.
 I fear we'll come tae harm.'

hoysed *hoisted* fee *wealth* gane *will suffice* white monie *silver*
half-fou *bushel* alake *alas* yestreen *last night*

21

Sir Patrick Spens

They hadna sailed a league, a league,
A league but barely three,
When the lift grew dark, and the wind blew loud,
And gurly grew the sea.

The anchors brak, and the topmasts lap,
It was sic a deadly storm;
And the waves cam oe'r the broken ship,
Till a' her sides were torn.

'O whaur will I get a guid sailor,
To take the helm in hand,
Till I get up to the tall top-mast,
Tae see if I can spy land?'

'O here am I, a sailor guid,
To take the helm in hand,
Till you got up tae the tall top-mast;
But I fear you'll ne'er spy land.'

He hadna gane a step, a step,
A step but barely ane,
When a bowt flew out o' oor goodly ship,
And the saut sea it came in.

'Gae fetch a web o' the silken claith,
Another o' the twine,
And wap them into our ship's side,
And let nae the sea cam in.'

They fetched a web o' the silken claith,
Another o' the twine,
And they wapp'd them round that guid ship's side,
But still the sea cam in.

lift *sky*   gurly *stormy, growly*   lap *sprang*   sic *such*   bowt *bolt*   saut *salt*
twine *coarse linen*   wap *bind, splice*

Sir Patrick Spens

O laith, laith, were our guid Scots lords
Tae wet their cork-heeled shoon!
But lang or a' the play was play'd,
They wet their hats aboon.

And mony was the feather bed,
That flatter'd on the faem;
And mony was the guid lord's son,
That never mair cam hame.

The ladies wrang their fingers white,
The maidens tore their hair,
A' for the sake o' their true loves;
For them they'll see nae mair.

O lang, lang, may the ladies sit,
Wi' the fans into their hand,
Before they see Sir Patrick Spens
Come sailing tae the strand!

And lang, lang, may the maidens sit,
With their gowd kaims in their hair,
A' waiting for their ain dear loves!
For them, they'll see nae mair.

Half-owre, half owre to Aberdour,
Tis fifty fathoms deep,
And there lies guid Sir Patrick Spens,
Wi' the Scots lords at his feet.

laith *loathe*   shoon *shoes*   or *before*   aboon *above*
flatter'd *floated*   kaims *combs*

23

Sir Patrick Spens

NOTES

The king needs a captain for his new ship and to take many Scots lords to Norway and fetch back the daughter of the king of that land – and is told that Sir Patrick Spens is the best skipper. It is during the winter, however, and only reluctantly does Sir Patrick agree to the mission. Once in Norway the local nobles complain that the Scots are costing them a fortune, despite the Scots bringing much treasure with them. In disgust the Scots leave but the ship is caught in a terrible gale. Despite his best efforts, Sir Patrick cannot save the ship and it is broken and sinks with the loss of all those on board.

This is apparently loosely based on events of 1290, although many of the details are contradictory. The Scots did go to Norway to retrieve the nine-year-old Margaret, known as the Maid of Norway and the daughter of the Norwegian king, although more importantly the granddaughter of Alexander III and at the time the last direct heir to the Scottish throne. The ship was not lost, however, and Margaret made it to Orkney, where unfortunately she died, reputedly from seasickness. In the poem it states that the king sits in Dunfermline toun, but Alexander III died in 1286 and Scotland had no king at the time of the mission.

Dunfermline has a royal palace, now a ruin, but there has been some discussion whether Sir Patrick left from Aberdour in Fife or from Aberdour in Aberdeenshire, which is some miles west of Fraserburgh. In favour of Aberdour in Fife is the closeness to Dunfermline, that the Spences were a Fife family (although from the East Neuk) and that travel by sea was usually quicker and easier than by land in the thirteenth century. The Aberdour in Aberdeenshire is a long way for many lords to come from Dunfermline. Just to confuse things slightly, however, is an alternative last verse:

O forty miles off Aberdeen,
Tis fifty fathoms deep,
And there lies guid Sir Patrick Spens
Wi' the Scots lords at his feet.

The ballad is from Child No 58.

The Border Widow's Lament

My love he built me a bonny bower,
And cled it a' wi' lily flower;
A bonnier bower ye ne'er did see,
Than my true love he built tae me.

There came a man by middle day,
He spied his sport and went away;
And brought the king that very night,
Who brak my bower and slew my knight.

He slew my knight tae me sae dear;
He slew my knight and poin'd his gear;
My servants a' for life did flee,
And left me in extremitie.

I sew'd his sheet, making my mane;
I watch'd the corpse, mysel alane;
I watch'd his body, night and day;
No living creature cam my way.

I took his body on my back,
And whiles I gaed and whiles I sat;
I digg'd a grave and laid him in,
And happ'd him wi' the sod sae green.

But think nae ye my heart was sair,
When I laid the mool on his yellow hair;
O think nae ye my heart was wae,
When I turn'd about awa' tae gae?

poin'd *confiscated, impounded* gear *property* making my mane *lamenting*
happ'd *covered* mool *earth, mould* wae *woe*

The Border Widow's Lament

Nae living man I'll love again,
Since that my lovely knight is slain;
Wi' ae lock o' his yellow hair
I'll chain my heart for evermair.

NOTES

A lady had a loving husband, a small laird, whom she deeply cared for in return. One day a servant of the king arrives, checks the whereabouts of the laird, and then brings the king to the laird's tower. The king has the laird hanged and takes all his property and land, leaving the lady destitute: even her servants have fled. The lady retrieves the corpse of her lord, cleans and prepares the body for burial, carries it on her back, and eventually buries it in a grave that she has had to dig herself. She then professes that no matter what happens she will never love another.

This ballad is believed to be based on the execution of William Cockburn of Henderland in 1530, who was beheaded for treason along with one of his neighbours, Adam Scott of Tushielaw, by James V (also see Johnie Armstrong). In the ballad, this takes place at his tower, but it appears he was taken to Edinburgh and there slain, his head being displayed at the city tolbooth.

Henderland was a small property with its own tower house (known as Cockburn's Tower) near Cappercleuch in the Borders, not far from St Mary's Loch; all that remains now is mound. Cockburn (along with many Borderers) was a reiver but he became notorious and so gained the attention of the authorities and eventual trial for treason. After his death, the story goes that his lady, perhaps called Margaret, despaired of life and tried to drown herself in the Henderland Burn at a place known as Lady's Seat. There are some remains of a burial ground and chapel on a hillock at Chapel Knowe, not far from the site of the tower, and this may be where the couple were buried. A reassembled broken slab is a memorial to one of the Cockburn lairds, although not to William.

Some of the verses in the ballad are similar to the longer 'The Lady Turned Serving Man', Child number 106.

Johnie Faa:
the Gypsy Laddie

The gypsies came tae oor guid lord's gate,
And wow but they sang sweetlie!
They sang sae sweet and sae very complete
That doun cam the fair lady.

And she cam tripping doun the stair,
And a' her maids before her;
As soon as they saw her weel-faired face,
They coost the glamour owre her.

'Gae tak frae me this gay mantle,
And bring tae me a plaidie;
For if kith and kin a' had sworn,
I'll follow the gipsy laddie.

'Yestreen I lay in a weel-made bed,
And my guid lord beside me;
This night I'll lie in a tenant's barn,
Whatever shall betide me.'

'Come tae your bed,' says Johnnie Faa,
'O come tae your bed, my dearie;
For I vow and I swear, by the hilt o' my sword,
That your lord sall nae mair come near ye.'

'I'll gae tae bed, tae my Johnnie Faa,
I'll gae tae my bed, my dearie;
For I vow and I swear, by what passed yestreen,
That my lord shall nae mair come near me.

weel-faired *good-looking*   coost *cast*   glamour *spell*
plaidie rough outer garment   yestreen *last night, yesterday evening*

Johnie Faa: the Gypsy Laddie

'I'll make a hap to my Johnnie Faa,
And I'll make a hap, my dearie;
And he's get a' the coat gaes round,
And my lord sall nae mair come near me.'

And when oor guid lord came home at een,
And speir'd for his fair lady,
The tane she cried, and the tither replied,
'She's awa' with the gipsy laddie.'

'Gae saddle tae me the black, black steed,
Gae saddle and make him ready;
Before that I either eat or sleep,
I'll gae seek my fair lady.'

And we were fifteen weel-made men,
Although we werenae bonnie;
And we were a' put doun for ane,
A fair young wanton lady.

hap *wrap* een *evening* speir'd *asked about*
put doun *killed, executed*

Cassillis House.

Johnie Faa: the Gypsy Laddie

NOTES

The lady of the castle hears the gypsies singing and is so taken with them (or – to be kinder – she has a spell cast on her) that she discards her fine clothing and comfortable life and runs off with them full willing. Her husband, however, arrives home and asks about the whereabouts of his wife; he is told that she is gone. He hurries after the gypsies, retrieves his wife, and has the gypsies put to death.

Some versions of the ballad suggest that the lady in question was the wife of the Earl of Cassillis, traditionally Lady Jean Hamilton who was married to John Kennedy, sixth Earl, in 1621. She was staying at what was then Cassillis Castle and Johnie Faa or Fall, the gypsy laddie, was her lover (gypsies, also known as Egyptians, were numerous in the border area of Scotland from the sixteenth century). The story goes that she was made to watch as Johnie and the other gypsies were hanged from the gallows tree, and even that her ghost still haunts the building, seen at one of the windows. Other locations for the story have been suggested as Culzean Castle or Maybole Castle, two other properties of the Earls of Cassillis. This alternative version makes no mention of a spell being cast on the lady.

In yet another version the lady suffers the same fate as the gypsies:

> 'Last night I lay on a fine feather bed,
> Wi' my guid lord beside me,
> This night I maun lie in the cold cold clay,
> Wi' the gypsies lying around me.'

Ballads and songs about respectable girls running away with the (sometimes raggle-taggle) gypsies are common throughout Britain and Europe. There is no evidence, incidentally, that Lady Jean Hamilton and John, Earl of Cassillis, were on anything but the best of terms, according to their own cordial correspondence of the time.

Cassillis House, which is still home to the Earls, lies about three miles north-east of Maybole in Ayrshire and dates from the thirteenth century.

Lord Randal

'O whaur hae ye been,
Lord Randal, my son?
And whaur hae ye been,
My handsome young man?'

'I hae been at the greenwood;
mother, mak my bed soon,
For I'm wearied wi' hunting,
And fain wad lie doun.'

'And wha met ye there,
Lord Randal, my son?
And wha met ye there,
My handsome young man?'

'O I met wi' my true love;
Mother, mak my bed soon,
For I'm wearied wi' hunting,
And fain wad lie doun.'

'And what did she gie ye,
Lord Randal, my son?
And what did she gie ye,
My handsome young man?'

'Eels fried in a pan;
Mother, mak my bed soon,
For I am wearied wi' hunting,
And fain wad lie doun.'

fain *must*   wearied *sickly, weak*

Lord Randal

'And wha gat your leavins,
    Lord Randal, my son?
And wha gat your leavins,
    My handsome young man?'

'My hawks and my hounds;
    Mother, mak my bed soon,
For I'm wearied wi' hunting,
    And fain wad lie doun.'

'And what becam o' them,
    Lord Randal, my son?
And what becam o' them,
    My handsome young man?'

'They stretch'd out their legs and died;
    Mother, mak my bed soon,
For I'm wearied wi' hunting,
    And fain wad lie doun.'

'O I fear you are poison'd,
    Lord Randal, my son!
I fear you are poison'd,
    My handsome young man!'

'O yes, I am poison'd;
    Mother, mak my bed soon,
For I'm sick at the heart,
    And I fain wad lie doun.'

'What d'ye leave tae your mother,
    Lord Randal, my son?
What d'ye leave tae your mother,
    My handsome young man?'

leavins *leftovers*

Lord Randal

'Four and twenty milk kye;
  Mother, mak my bed soon,
  For I'm sick at the heart,
  And I fain would lie doun.'

'What d'ye leave tae your sister,
  Lord Randal, my son?
What d'ye leave tae your sister,
  My handsome young man?'

'My gowd and my siller;
  Mother, mak my bed soon,
  For I'm sick at the heart,
  And I fain wad lie doun.'

'What d'ye leave tae your brother,
  Lord Randal, my son?
What d'ye leave tae your brother,
  My handsome young man?'

'My houses and my lands;
  Mother, mak my bed soon,
  For I'm sick at the heart,
  And I fain wad lie doun.'

'What d'ye leave tae your true love,
  Lord Randal, my son?
What d'ye leave tae your true love,
  My handsome young man?'

'I leave her hell and fire;
  Mother, mak my bed soon,
  For I'm sick at the heart,
  And I fain wad lie doun.'

kye *cattle*

Lord Randal

NOTES

Lord Randal returns one day from hunting, telling his mother that he is sickly and must go to bed. His mother asks him what he had been doing: he tells her he met his lover in the woods and she cooked for him a dish of eels. When his hawks and his hounds ate the leftovers they sickened and died, and it soon becomes clear that Lord Randal has been poisoned. His mother goes on to ask what he is going to leave to various members of the family, and he tells her of the legacies, until he get to his true love, when he leaves her hell and fire, for it is she who has poisoned him.

This ballad is found in several versions, including 'Lord Ronald', except in it Lord Ronald bequeaths his love a more earthly punishment:

> 'What'll ye leave tae your sweetheart,
> Lord Ronald, my son?
> What'll ye leave tae your sweetheart,
> My handsome young man?
>
> 'I'll leave her a rope,
> And a high gallows tree,
> And let her hang there,
> For the poisoning o' me!'

The mention of the greenwood in the first verse hints that Lord Randal was doing more than just hunting with his true love – the green wood was a prime location for conceiving a male child. 'Wearied' in this context means sickly or weak, rather than just tired. Eel blood is poisonous but cooking the eel properly (or even the act of digestion) should destroy the toxin.

One story is that the ballad is based on the death of Randolph, Earl of Chester, in 1232, who was reputedly poisoned by his wife, but there are similar ballads from many parts of Europe.

The ballad is from Child No 12.

Johnie Armstrong

Some speaks o' lords, some speaks o' lairds,
And sic like men o' high degree;
Of a gentleman I sing a sang,
Some time call'd laird o' Gilnockie.

The king he writes a loving letter,
Wi' his ain had sae tenderlie;
And he hath sent it tae Johnie Armstrong,
Tae cam and speak wi' him speedilie.

The Elliots and Armstrongs did convene,
They were a gallant companie;
'We'll ride and meet our lawfu' king,
And bring him safe tae Gilnockie.'

'Mak kinnen and capon ready, then,
And venison in great plentie;
We'll welcome hame our royal king;
I hope he'll dine at Gilnockie!'

They ran their horse on the Langholm houm,
And brak their spears with meikle main;
The ladys lookit frae their loft-windows,
'God bring oor men weil back again!'

When Johnie cam before the king,
Wi' all his men sae brave tae see,
The king he movit his bonnet tae him;
He ween'd he was king as well as he.

kinnen *rabbit* houm *flat area beside a river* main *force*
movit *took off* ween'd *thought, surmised*

Johnie Armstrong

'May I find grace, my sovereign liege,
　　Grace for my loyal men and me?
　For my name is Johnie Armstrong,
And subject o' yours, my liege,' said he.

　'Awa', awa', thou traitor strang!
　Out o' my sight thou mayst soon be!
　　I grantit ne'er a traitor's life,
　　And I'll nae begin with thee.'

'Grant me my life, my liege, my king,
　And a bonny gift I will give tae thee;
Full four and twenty milk-white steeds,
　Were a' foal'd in a year tae me.

'I'll gie thee all these milk-white steeds,
　That prance and nicher at a speir,
　　Wi' as meikle good Inglis gilt
And four o' their braid backs dow beir.'

　'Awa', awa', thou traitor strang!
　Out o' my sight thou mayst soon be!
　　I grantit ne'er a traitor's life,
　And now I'll nae begin with thee.'

'Grant me my life, my liege, my king,
　And a bonny gift I'll gie thee,
Good four-and twenty ganging mills,
　That gang throw a' the year tae me.

'These four-and-twenty mills complete
Sall gang for thee through all the year,
　And as meikle of guid red wheat
　As their happers dow tae bear.'

strang *strong*　nicher *neigh*　speir *request*　Inglis gilt *English gold*
ganging *working*　happers dow tae bear *hoppers can contain*

Johnie Armstrong

'Awa', awa', thou traitor strang!
Out o' my sight thou mayst soon be!
I grantit ne'er a traitor's life,
And now I'll nae begin with thee.'

'Grant me my life, my liege, my king,
And I great gift I'll gie tae thee;
Bold four-and-twenty sisters' sons,
Sall for thee fecht, though all should be flee.'

'Awa', awa', thou traitor strang!
Out o' my sight thou mayst soon be!
I grantit ne'er a traitor's life,
And now I'll nae begin with thee.'

'Grant me my life, my liege, my king,
And a brave gift I'll gie tae thee,
A' between here and Newcastle toun
Sall pay their yearly rent tae thee.'

'Awa', awa', thou traitor strang!
Out o' my sight thou mayst soon be!
I grantit ne'er a traitor's life,
And now I'll nae begin with thee.'

'Ye lied, ye lied, now, king,' he says,
'Although a king and prince ye be,
For I lov'd nothing in a' my life,
I dare well say it, but honestlie;

'But a fat horse, and a fair woman,
Twa bonny dogs tae kill a deer:
But Ingland should hae found me meal and malt,
If I hae lived this hundred year!

fecht *fight* fat *well fed* Ingland *England*
found me *supplied me with*

36

Johnie Armstrong

'She sall found me meal and malt,
And beef and mutton in a' plenty;
But ne'er a Scots wife could hae said
That ere I skaith'd her a pure flie.

'Tae seek hot water beneath cold ice,
Surely is a great follie;
I have ask'd grace at a graceless face,
But there is nane for my men and me.

'But had I ken'd or I cam frae hame,
How thou unkind wadst been tae me,
I wad have kept the border-side,
In spite of a' thy force and thee.

'Wist Ingland's king that I wae ta'en,
O gin a blyth man wad he be!
For ance I slew his sister's son,
And on his breast-bane brak a tree.'

Johnie wore a girdle about his middle.
Embroidered owre wi' burning gold,
Bespangled wi' the same metal,
Most beautiful was tae behold.

There hang nine targats at Johnie's hat,
And ilk ane worth three-hundred pound:
'What wants that knave that a should have,
But the sword o' honour and the crown!

'O whaur gat thou these targats, Johnie,
That blink sae brawly abune thy brie?'
'I gat them in the field fechting,
Where, cruel king, thou durstna be!

skaith'd her a pure flie *did her any harm* or ere, *before* unkind *excessively harsh*
kept *defended* wist *knew* blyth *joyous* ance *once* tree *spear*
targat *shield-shaped ornament* blink *sparkle* brie *brow* durstna *dare not*

Johnie Armstrong

'Had I my horse, and my harness good,
And riding as I wont tae be,
It should have been told this hundred year
The meeting of my king and me.

'God be with thee, Kirsty, my brother,
Lang live thou laird of Mangertoun!
Lang mayst thou live on the border-side
Or thou se thy brother ride up and doun.

'God be with thee, Kirsty, my son,
Whaur thou sits on my nurse's knee!
But and thou live this hundred year,
Thy father's better thou'lt never be.

'Farewell, my bonny Gilnock-Hall,
Whaur on Esk-side thou standest stout!
If I hae liv'd but seven years mair,
I wad have gilt thee round about.'

John murder'd was at Carlinrigg,
And all his gallant companie;
But Scotland's heart was never sae wae,
Tae see sae mony brave man die.

Because they had sav'd their country dear,
Frae Inglishmen; nane were sae bold,
While Johnie liv'd on the border-side,
Nane of them durst cam near his hold.

but and *but if*   wae *woe, sad*   hold *castle, stronghold*

38

Johnie Armstrong

NOTES

Johnie Armstrong of Gilnockie is one of the leaders of the powerful Armstrongs and Elliots who, although maintaining the border lands against the English, are also notorious for raiding, reiving and following no orders but those given by their own leaders. The king, however, sends Johnie a letter of friendship, suggesting they should meet. Johnie goes with his men, thinking that he will be safe, but the king actually intends to execute Johnie and his party, and has lured him under false pretences. Johnie tries to bargain for his life, offering the king horses or mills or even the rents of all the properties of the border as far as Newcastle. He also tells the king that, although he has stolen from the English, he has never harmed his own country and has defended Scotland. When it becomes clear that the king will not be swayed, Johnie rebukes the king, saying that his wealth has been gained from fighting the English, a thing that the king has not dared to do, and how happy the English will be that Johnie is gone. Finally, he says farewell and he is hanged along with his men.

This ballad is based on the execution of Johnie Armstrong of Gilnockie and his men by James V in 1530 (also see the Border Widow's Lament). According to some sources, Johnie was tricked into joining the king when sent what seemed like a friendly letter, although others suggest he was merely ambushed by the king. Johnie was not, however, quite the hero made out in the ballad and was a notorious reiver, making numerous raids into England. Nor was Gilnockie quite the impregnable fortress suggested, as it had been burnt by the English some seven years before in 1523. Nevertheless it was most likely bad faith, at best, by James V and militarily foolish, as the Armstrongs had helped maintain the border against the English, in spite of their unruliness. When James went to war in 1542 at the Battle of Solway Moss, the Armstrongs did not join his forces and he was humiliatingly defeated; he died shortly afterwards, leaving the newly born Mary, Queen of Scots as his heir.

The site of Gilnockie (or Gilnock Hall) is two miles north of Canonbie on the west side of the Scottish Borders, just south of the River Esk, while Hollows Tower, a later stronghold of the Armstrongs, is nearby. This tower has been rerooted and houses the Clan Armstrong Centre. At Carlanrig, the site of the execution and where Johnie and his followers were buried in a mass grave, there is a stone memorial; this is located off the main A7 road, about seven or so miles south-west of Hawick. Mangerton, of which little now survives, was the main castle of the Armstrongs and stood a mile south of Newcastleton, also in the borders. John 'Black Jock' Armstrong, from this branch of the family, was also executed in 1530.

The ballad is from Child No 73.

The Gay Goss Hawk

'O weel's me o' my gay goss hawk,
That he can speak and flee;
He'll carry a letter tae my love,
Bring back another tae me.'

'O how and I your true-love ken,
Or how can I her know?
When frae her mouth I ne'er heard couth,
Nor wi' my eyes her saw.'

'O weel sall ye my true-love ken,
As soon as you her see;
For, o' a' the flowers in Ingland,
The fairest flower is she.

'At even at my love's bower door,
There grows a bowing birk,
And sit ye doun and sing thereon,
As she gangs tae the kirk.

'An four-and-twenty ladies fair,
Will wash and gae tae kirk,
But well sall ye my true-love ken.
For she wears gowd upon her skirt.

'And four-and-twenty gay ladies,
Will tae the mass repair,
But weel sall ye my true-love ken,
For she wears gowd in her hair.'

goss *friendly, crony*   weel's me o' *it's fortunate for me concerning*
couth *speech*   birk *birch*   kirk *church*

The Gay Goss Hawk

O even at the lady's bower door,
There grows a bowing birk,
And she sat doun and sang thereon,
As she gaed tae the kirk.

'O eat and drink, my marys a',
The wine flows you among,
Till I gang tae my shot-window,
And hear yon bonny bird's song.

'Sing on, sing on, my bonny bird,
The song ye sang yestreen,
For I ken by your high singin',
You're frae my true-love sent.'

O first he sang a merry song,
And then he sang a grave,
And then he peck'd his feathers grey,
Tae her the letter gave.

'Ha, there's a letter frae your love,
He says he sent ye three,
He canna wait your love langer,
But for your sake he'll die.

'He bids you write a letter tae him;
He says he's sent you five;
He canna wait your love langer,
Tho' you're the fairest woman alive.'

'Ye bid him bake his bridal-bread,
And brew his bridal-ale,
And I'll meet him in fair Scotland,
Lang, lang or it be stale.'

marys *maids* shot-window *hinged window*
yestreen *yesterday evening or before*

The Gay Goss Hawk

She's doen her tae her father dear,
Fa'en low doun on her knee;
'A boon, a boon, my father dear,
I pray you, grant it me.'

'Ask on, ask on, my dochter,
And granted it sall be;
Except ae squire in fair Scotlan',
And him ye sall ne'er see.'

'The only boon, my father dear,
That I do crave o' thee,
Is gin I die in southern lands,
In Scotlan' tae bury me.

'And the firstin kirk that ye cam till,
Ye gar the bells be rung,
And the nextin kirk ye cam till,
Ye gar the mass be sung.

'And the thirdin kirk that ye cam tae,
You deal gowd for my sake,
And the fourthin kirk ye cam tae,
You tarry there till night.'

She is doen tae her bigly bower,
As fast as she could fare,
And she has ta'en a sleepy draught,
That she hae mix'd wi' care.

She laid doun upon her bed,
And soon she's fa'en asleep,
And soon owre every tender limb,
Cold death began tae creep.

doen her *gone* fa'en *fallen* dochter *daughter* gin *if*
gar *get (make happen)* bigly *fine*

42

The Gay Goss Hawk

When night was flown and day was come,
Nae ane that did her see,
But thought that she was surely dead,
As ony lady could be.

Her father and her brothers dear,
Gar make tae her a bier;
The tae half was guid red gowd,
The tither o' siller clear.

Her mother and her sisters fair,
Gar work for her a sark;
The tae half was o' cambrick fine,
The tither o' needle wark.

The firstin kirk they cam till,
They gar the bells be rung,
And the nextin kirk they cam tae,
They gar the mass be sung.

The thirdin kirk they cam tae,
The dealt gowd for her sake,
And the fourthin kirk they cam tae,
Lo, there they met her make!

'Lay doun, lay doun the bigly bier,
Let me the dead look on.'
Wi' cherry cheeks and ruby lips,
She lay and smil'd on him.

'O ae sheave o' your bread, true-love,
And ae glass o' your wine,
For I hae fast'd for your sake,
These fully days is nine.

sark *shift or shirt (burial garment)*   make *mate or love*
sheave *slice*

The Gay Goss Hawk

'Gang hame, gang hame, my seven bold brothers,
  Gang hame and sound your horn;
And you may boast in southern lands,
  Your sister's play'd you scorn.'

play'd you scorn *made a fool of you*

NOTES

A Scottish lord and an English lady have fallen in love; the lord, however, has heard no word from his love for some time. So he sends off his friendly (speaking) hawk, first telling the bird how to recognise his love by her beauty and the amount of gold in which she is arrayed. The hawk flies off and finds the lady, letting her know that the lord is sickening and will die soon if she does not come to him; he has sent her numerous letters, none of which she has received. The lady goes to her father and he forbids her from any meeting, but she gets him to promise that, if she dies, she will be buried in Scotland and that they must go on until they reach the fourth church. Retiring to her bower, she takes a potion and appears to have died. So her family carry out her last wishes and take her body to Scotland where they stop for the night at the fourth church. Here, the lady's love appears and she comes back from apparent death and the two lovers are reunited. She then tells her seven brothers to return home, for she has tricked them.

A ballad with a happy ending: there are a few!

The ballad is from Child No 96.

44

Marie Hamilton

Marie Hamilton's tae the kirk gane,
Wi' ribbons in her hair;
The king thought mair o' Marie Hamilton
Than ony that were there.

Marie Hamilton's tae the kirk gane
Wi' ribbons on her breast;
The king thought mair o' Marie Hamilton
Than he listen'd tae the priest.

Marie Hamilton's tae the kirk gane,
Wi' gloves upon her hands;
The king thought mair o' Marie Hamilton
Than the queen and a' her lands.

She hadna been about the king's court
A month, but barely ane,
Till she was beloved by a' the king's court,
And the king the only man.

She hadna been about the king's court
A month, but barely three,
Till frae the king's court Marie Hamilton,
Marie Hamilton durstna be.

The king is tae the abbey gane,
To pu' the abbey tree,
To scale the babe frae Marie's heart;
But the thing it wadna be.

durstna *dare not*   pu' *pull (fruit from a tree)*
scale *drive away, get rid of*

45

Marie Hamilton

O she has roll'd it in her apron,
And set it on the sea.
'Gae sink ye or swim ye, bonny babe,
Ye'se get nae mair o' me.'

Word is tae the kitchen gane,
And word is to the ha',
And word is tae the noble room
Amang the ladies a',
That Marie Hamilton's brought tae bed,
And the bonny babe's miss'd and awa'.

Scarcely had she lain doun again,
And scarcely fa'en asleep,
When up and started our guid queen
Just at her bed-feet;
Saying, 'Marie Hamilton, whaur's your babe?
For I am sure I heard it greet.'

'O nae, o nae, my noble queen!
Think nae sic thing tae be;
Twas but a stitch intae my side,
And sair it troubles me!'

'Get up, get up, Marie Hamilton:
Get up and follow me;
For I am gang to Edinburgh toun,
A rich wedding for tae see.'

O slowly, slowly rase she up,
And slowly put she on;
And slowly rade she out the way
Wi' mony a weary groan.

roll'd *wrapped, rolled*   greet *wail, cry*

Marie Hamilton

The queen was clad in scarlet
Her merry maids a' in green;
And every toun that they cam tae,
They took Marie for the queen.

'Ride hooly, hooly, gentlemen,
Ride hooly now wi' me!
For ne'er, I am sure, a wearier burd
Rade in your companie.'

But little wist Marie Hamilton,
When she rade on the broun,
That she was gaen tae Edinburgh toun,
And a' tae be put doun.

'Why weep ye sae, ye burgess wives,
Why look yae sae on me?
O I am gang to Edinburgh toun,
A rich wedding for tae see.'

When she gaed up the tolbooth stairs,
The corks frae her heels did flee;
And lang oe'r she cam doun again,
She was condemn'd tae die.

When she cam to the Netherbow Port,
She laugh'd loud laughters three;
But when she cam to the gallows foot
The tears blinded her e'e.

'Yestreen the queen had four Maries,
This night she'll hae but three;
There was Mary Seton, and Marie Beaton,
And Marie Carmichael, and me.

hooly *gently, rolled* e'e *eyes* wist *understood* put doun *killed*
yestreen *yesterday evening, last night*

47

Marie Hamilton

'O often have I dress'd my queen,
And I've put gowd upon her hair;
But now I've gotten for my reward
The gallows tae be my share.

'Often have I dressed my queen
And often made her bed;
But now I've gotten for my reward
The gallows tree tae tread.

'I charge ye all ye mariners,
When ye sail owre the faem,
Let neither my father nor mother get wit
But that I'm coming hame.

'I charge ye all ye mariners,
That sail upon the sea,
That neither my father nor mother get wit
The dog's death I am to die.

'For if my father and mother got wit,
And my bold brethren three,
O mickle wad be the guid red blude,
This day wad be spilt for me!

'O little did my mother ken,
The day she cradl'd me,
The lands I was tae travel in
Or the death I was tae die!'

mickle *much, large amount* die is pronounced 'dee'
ken *know*

Marie Hamilton

NOTES

Marie Hamilton is one of the ladies-in-waiting to the queen but she has an affair with the king, the result of which is that she becomes pregnant. When the baby is born, she leaves it to die by abandoning it on the sea and she hopes that nobody knows that she was with child. But word has already spread, despite her denials, and the queen commands her to come with her to Edinburgh. Although still weak from the birth, Marie accompanies her – but once in Edinburgh Marie is accused of infanticide and is sentenced to be executed by hanging.

An alternative name for the ballad is 'The Four Maries'. The queen in question is usually thought to be Mary, Queen of Scots, and Marie Hamilton to be one of the four companions of Mary, known as the Four Maries. In the story Marie has been made pregnant by Henry Stewart, Lord Darnley, Mary's husband. The usually pronunciation of Marie's name is 'Mairi', the Gaelic for Mary. The mention in the ballad of the 'abbey tree' is probably a reference to a herb which could induce an abortion, although in this case it does not work.

The historical Four Maries were actually Mary Fleming, Mary Livingston, Mary Seton and Mary Beaton (not Hamilton or Carmichael), and none of them were ever accused of infanticide. In 1563, however, a French woman at the court of Mary was executed for killing her baby, along with her lover, which may be the origin of the ballad. It is certainly true that Lord Darnley was a philanderer, and had a reputation for affairs with both women (and men) but he was not implicated. In the ballad and despite her heinous crime there is sympathy for Marie, and it is the death of her baby, and not her promiscuity, that condemns her. Her lover, however, receives no punishment, despite him being responsible for her unhappy predicament.

In 1719 at the court of Peter the Great in Russia a beautiful young woman called Mary Hamilton, who had had an affair with the Czar, was beheaded for murdering her baby after birth. This Mary had been maid-of-honour to the Czarina Catherine, and it is said that her head was spiked and put on display after the execution.

It seems likely that these two events have been conflated into the ballad.

The ballad is Child No 173 and is not on record before 1790.

Lord Thomas and Lady Margaret

Lord Thomas, he was a guid lord's son;
Lady Margaret, she lov'd him weel,
And for the sake o' guid Lord Thomas,
Lady Margaret she's gane wild.

He call'd up his merry men a',
By ane, by twa, by three;
Saying, 'Gae and hunt this wild woman,
Mony a mile frae me.'

They hunt'd her high, they hunt'd her low,
They hunt'd her owre the plain,
Till the petticoat o' scarlet Lady Margaret wore,
Could ne'er be wore again.

She look'd high, and she look'd laigh,
And she look'd round again,
And there she saw a braw Scots lord
Come riding owre the plain.

'Some help, some help, my guid lord,' she said;
'Some help pray gae tae me;
I am a lady that's deeply in love,
And banish'd frae my ain countrie.'

'Nae help, nae help, Lady Margaret,' he said.
'Nae help I gie tae thee;
Until you forsake a' the men in the world,
My ain wedded bride tae be!'

laigh *low*

Lord Thomas and Lady Margaret

'I'll forsake a' the men in the world,
By ane, by twa, by three;
I will forsake a' the men in the world,
Your ain wedded bride tae be.'

Lady Margaret sat in her bower window,
A silken seam sew'd she;
And there she saw her good Lord Thomas,
In beggar's garb was he.

'Some help, some help, Lady Margaret,
Some help come show tae me,
Or wi' my broad sword I'll kill your lord,
And my ain wedded bride you'll be!'

'O God forbid, Lord Thomas,' she said.
'That ony sic thing should be,
For I've twenty casks in my cellar,
And ye'se taste them a' wi' me.'

She call'd for her butler boy,
Tae draw her a pint o' wine,
And wi' her fingers lang and sma'
She steer'd the poison in.

She put it tae her rosie cheeks,
Syne tae her dimpl'd chin;
She put it tae her ruby lips,
But ne'er a drop went in.

He put it tae his rosie cheeks,
Syne tae his dimpl'd chin;
He put it tae his ruby lips,
And the rank poison gaed in.

sic *such*   syne *next, directly after*

Lord Thomas and Lady Margaret

'Tak awa' your wine, Lady Margaret,
For o' it I am wearie.'—
'And sae was I o' your hounds, Lord Thomas,
When ye hunt'd them after me.'

'But I will bury ye as decentlie,' said she;
'As ony o' your kin,
And I will tell my wedded lord,
That you are my sister's son.'

wearie *sickly, weak*

NOTES

Lord William and Lady Margaret apparently love each other, but she flees into the countryside to escape from him – the reason why is not made clear, although it possible they are closely related, perhaps nephew and aunt. Lord William tries to find Margaret by hunting her with dogs and she is chased sorely, but finds redemption when she meets a new lord. She agrees to marry this new fellow, forsaking all other men, including Lord Thomas. Later, Lord Thomas arrives dressed as a beggar, threatening to slay Margaret's husband so he can marry her. She, however, offers Thomas some poisoned wine and, while she avoids drinking it, he is fatally poisoned.

There are at least two major different versions of this ballad (Child, no 260), but neither make it clear why Lord William suddenly decides to hunt Lady Margaret with dogs…

Bessie Bell and Mary Gray

O Bessie Bell and Mary Gray,
They were twa bonnie lasses;
They biggit a bower on yon burn-brae,
And theekit it o'er wi' rashes.

They theekit it o'er wi' rushes green,
They theekit it o'er wi' heather;
But the pest cam frae the burghs-toun,
And slew them baith taegither.

They thought tae lie in Methven kirkyard,
Amang their noble kin;
But they maun lie in Stronach haugh,
To biek fornent the sin.

And Bessie Bell and Mary Gray,
They were twa bonnie lasses;
They biggit a bower on yon burn-brae,
And theekit it o'er with rashes.

biggit *built*   rashes rushes   theekit *thatched*   pest *plague*
haugh *water mead*   biek *bake*   fornent *in front of*   sin *sun*

NOTES
Bessie Bell and Mary Gray were two great friends, who built a bower together on a flat above a burn. The plague comes from the town and both girls are afflicted and die. Because of the terrible illness, nobody will come near their corpses so they can be buried in Methven kirkyard. They are left to bake in the sun until only their bones are left.

   In as far as it is possible to be certain, Bessie (Elizabeth) Bell and Mary Gray are believed to be two historical figures and to have

Bessie Bell and Mary Gray

died in 1645 (or 1666) from the plague. Bessie (in some versions Betsy) Bell was the daughter of the laird of Kinvaird, a property five or so miles north and west of Perth, and she was friends with Mary Gray of Lynedoch. Lynedoch lies some miles away, near Methven. Bessie was visiting Mary at Lynedoch when they caught plague, apparently from the same young man from Perth whom they both admired and who brought them food but caught plague himself and then infected them.

The girls had built a bower, about quarter of a mile west of Lynedoch House, and there remained during their illness and then death. After a suitable time (when their remains were no longer believed to be infectious having been entirely defleshed), they were buried on Burn Brae, their graves now surrounded by a stone wall and iron railings.

In truth, it seems more likely that, should the events be true, the two girls were buried in properly consecrated ground, either in Methven kirkyard or elsewhere.

This ballad is from Child 201, and is also known as 'The Twa Lasses'.

Lady Jean

The king's young dochter was sittin' in her window,
  Sewin' at her fine silken seam,
She look'd out at her braw bower window,
  And she saw the leaves growin' green.

She stack her needle intae her sleeve,
  Her seam doun by her tae,
And she is awa' tae the merry green wood,
  For tae pu' the nuts and slaes.

She had nae pu'd a nut at a',
  A nut by scarcely three,
Till out and spak a braw young man,
  Saying how durst thou bow this tree.

'It's I will pu' these nuts,' she said;
  'And I will bow this tree,
And I will cam tae the merry green wood,
  And ask nae leave of thee.'

He took her by the middle sae sma',
  And laid her on the grass sae green,
And he has ta'en his will o' her,
  And he let her up again.

'Now since ye have got your will o' me,
  Pray tell tae me your name;
For I am the king's young dochter,' she said;
  'And this night I durstna gae hame.'

dochter daughter   pu' *pick, pull*   slaes *sloes*   braw *fine, splendid*
  durst *dare*   bow *bend*

55

Lady Jean

'If ye be the king's young dochter,' he said;
  'I am his auldest son;
I wish I had died on some distant isle,
  And ne'er had cam hame.

'The first time I cam hame, Jeanie,
  Thou werenae here nor born,
I wish my pretty ship had sunk,
  And I had ne'er return'd.

'The next time I cam hame, Jeanie,
  Thou was sitting on thy nurse's knee,
And I wiss my pretty ship had sunk,
  And I had seen ne'er thee.

'And the next time I cam hame, Jeanie,
  I met thee here alane,
I wish I had died on some distant isle,
  And ne'er had cam hame.'

She put her hand doun by her side,
  Doun intae her spare,
And she pu'd out a wee pen knife,
  And she woundit hersel fu' sair.

Slowlie, slowlie, rose she up,
  And slowlie gaed she hame,
Until she cam tae her father's parlour,
  And there she did sigh and mane.

'O sister, sister, mak my bed,
  O' the clean linen and straw;
O sister, sister, mak my bed,
  Doun in the parlour below.'

wiss *wish* spare *gap in her gown* mane *moan*

Lady Jean

And her father, he cam tripping doun the stairs,
He steps they were fu' slow,
'I think, I think, Lady Jean,' he said,
'Ye're lying far owre low.'

'O late last night as I cam hame,
Doun by yonder castle wa',
O heavy, heavy was the stane,
That on my breast did fa'.'

Her mother, she cam doun the stair,
Her steps they were fu' slow,
'I think, I think, Lady Jean,' she said,
'Ye're lying far owre low.'

'O late last night as I cam hame,
Doun by yonder castle wa',
O heavy, heavy was the stane,
That on my breast did fa'.'

Her sister cam tripping doun the stair,
Her steps they were fu' slow,
'I think, I think, Lady Jean,' she said,
'Ye're lying far owre low.'

'O late last night as I cam hame,
Doun by yonder castle wa',
O heavy, heavy was the stane,
That on my breast did fa'.''

Her brother, he cam tripping doun the stair,
His steps they were fu' slow,
He sank intae his sister's arms,
And they died as white as snow

Lady Jean

NOTES

Lady Jean is in her bower sewing when she decides to go to the woods to collect nuts and berries. Here she is confronted by a man, who asks how she dares to pick from the trees; she responds by saying because she does. He then takes her, lays her on the grass and has sex with her. When he his finished, she asks to know his name and they find out that they are brother and sister. The brother, who is much older than her, has been abroad, and the last time he saw his sister she was only a young child. Lady Jean takes out a knife and stabs herself and then returns home to her castle, mortally wounded. Her parents and sister come to see her, and then her brother, who lies beside her and dies himself – perhaps of a broken heart.

In some commentaries, it is suggested that Lady Jean is raped by her brother, but there is nothing in this version to suggest that, although Lady Jean does say she dares not go home, presumably because she may be pregnant. Indeed, that she goes to the green wood suggests that she has more than collecting fruit on her mind. That they have inadvertently committed incest is what drives her to suicide, not that she has been ravished. Indeed, the ballad is not critical of the nature of the relationship.

Incestuous relationships are implied in a number of ballads, the result of being brought up separately and siblings being of different ages. A similar ballad, called 'Rosianne', has Rosianne telling her father, mother and sister that she has been made pregnant by her brother. In this ballad, her brother stabs and kills her. The brother then flees abroad and does not appear to be properly punished for his crime.

This ballad is from Child 52 and is also known as 'The King's Dochter Lady Jean'. There are at least four versions of this ballad, and in two of these it does suggest that the lady in question was forced.

Edward

'Why does your brand sae drop wi' blude,
Edward, Edward?
Why does your brand sae drop wi' blude?
And why sae sad gang ye, O?'

'O I hae kill'd my hawk sae guid,
Mither, mither;
O I hae kill'd my hawk sae guid,
And I hae nae mair but he, O.'

'Your hawk's blude was ne'er sae red,
Edward, Edward;
Your hawk's blude was ne'er sae red,
My dear son, I tell thee, O.'

'O I hae kill'd my red-roan steed,
Mither, mither;
O I hae kill'd my red-roan steed,
That ere was ae fair and free, O.'

'Your steed was auld, and ye hae got mair,
Edward, Edward;
Your steed was auld, and ye hae got mair;
Some other dule ye dree, O?'

'O I hae kill'd my father dear,
mither, mither;
O I hae kill'd my father dear,
Alas and wae is me, O!'

brand *sword* roan *variegated colours*
dule ye dree *grief you suffer*

Edward

'And whatten penance will ye dree for that,
    Edward, Edward?
Whatten penance will ye dree for that?
    My dear son, now tell me, O.'

'I'll set my feet in yonder boat,
    Mither, mither;
I'll set my feet in yonder boat,
    And I'll fare o'er the sea, O.'

'And what will ye do wi' your towers and your ha',
    Edward, Edward?
And what will ye do wi' your towers and your ha',
    That were sae fair tae see, O?'

'I'll let them stand till they doun fa',
    Mither, mither;
I'll let them stand till they doun fa',
    For here ne'er mair maun I be, O.'

'And what will ye leave tae your bairns and your wife,
    Edward, Edward?
And what will ye leave tae your bairns and your wife,
    When ye gang owre the sea, O?'

'The world's room: let them beg through life,
    mither, mither;
The world's room: let them beg through life;
    For them ne'er mair will I see, O.'

'And what will ye leave tae your ain mither dear,
    Edward, Edward?
And what will ye leave tae your mother dear,
    My dear son, now tell me, O?'

dree *suffer*   maun *must*

Edward

'The curse o' hell frae me sall ye bear,
  mither, mither;'
The curse o' hell frae me sall ye bear:
  Sic counsels ye gave tae me, O!'

sic *such*

NOTES

Edward returns home, and his mother asks him why his sword is begored in blood. At first he claims he has killed his hawk and then his horse, but then he admits he has murdered his father and that he must flee. His mother asks to whom he is going to leave his property and how his wife and children will survive, but he gives no answer other than to predict they will have to beg. Then she asks what he is going to leave to her, and he replies the curse of hell because he killed his father because of her advice.

This ballad is from Child 13, and there are many similar versions, including 'Son David', although in that ballad it is the brother who is slain and the mother is not to blame. In structure 'Edward' also has much in common with 'Lord Randal'.

Helen of Kirkconnel

I wish I were whaur Helen lies,
Night and day on me she cries;
O that I were whaur Helen lies,
On fair Kirkconnel lea!

Curst be the heart that thought the thought,
And curst be the hand that fired the shot,
When in my arms bird Helen dropp'd,
And died tae succour me!

O think nae ye my love was sair,
When my love dropp'd and spak nae mair!
There did she swoon wi' meikle care,
On fair Kirkconnel Lea.

As I went doun tae the water side,
None but my foe tae be my guide,
None but my foe tae be my guide,
On fair Kirkconnel Lea.

I light'd down my sword tae draw,
I hack'd him intae pieces sma'
I hack'd him intae pieces sma',
For her sake that died for me.

O Helen fair, beyond compare!
I'll mak a garland o' thy hair,
Sall bind my heart for evermair,
Until the day I die!

meikle *much, a lot*

Helen of Kirkconnel

O that I were where Helen lies!
Night and day on me she cries;
Out o' my bed she bids me rise,
Says, 'Haste, and come tae me!'

O Helen fair! O Helen chaste!
If I were with thee, I'd be blest,
Whaur thou lies low and taks thy rest,
On fair Kirkconnel Lea.

I wish my grave were growing green,
A winding-sheet drawn owre my e'en,
And I in Helen's arms lying,
On fair Kirkconnel Lea.

I wish I were where Helen lies!
Night and day on me she cries;
And I am weary o' the skies,
For her sake that died for me.

e'en *eyes*

NOTES

Helen of Kirkconnel, a fair and chaste lass, is in love with the narrator of the ballad. A rejected suitor tries to shoot Helen's lover but she takes the bullet and dies. The narrator of the ballad then pursues the shooter and hacks him into small pieces with his sword. The narrator then professes of his undying love for fair Helen, that he wishes that he was also dead and in a grave beside her.

The story is set around the middle of the sixteenth century and the heroine was Helen Irvine of Kirkconnel, being a property a few miles east of Ecclefechan in Dumfriesshire. Helen was with her love, Adam Fleming, and the two were enjoying each other's company by the banks of the Kirtle Water. A rejected suitor, Richard Bell of Blacket House, tried to shoot Fleming but only managed to kill Helen, who bravely stepped in front of her lover. Fleming then rushed Bell and cut him to pieces. Fearing reprisals, no doubt, from the vengeful Bells, Fleming fled Scotland for Spain and on returning went to Helen's grave in Kirkconnel kirkyard and, lying on her tombstone, died himself and was buried beside her. A garland or lock of hair is a motif for undying eternal love and is used in several ballads.

In Kirkconnel graveyard (the church is very ruinous), which lies on the east bank of the Kirtle Water, is a stone memorial carved with a sword which formerly had an inscription with 'Adam Fleming', although this has now gone. The story goes that this is the Fleming of the ballad and he was buried alongside Helen. The place where Helen was reputedly shot is marked by a cross, some nine-foot high, known as Fair Helen's Cross.

There was a tower house at Kirkconnel, south of the church, but nothing remains, and there was also a village here, believed to have been abandoned and destroyed because of an outbreak of plague. Indeed, Fair Helen's Cross may have been the market cross of Kirkconnel which was re-erected at its present site. The reduced ruin of Blacket House, said to be the home of Helen's killer, stands about 0.5 miles south-west of Kirkconnel, on the west bank of the Kirtle Water.

The ballad is from Sir Walter Scott's *The Minstrelsy of the Scottish Border*, published in 1802, and is also known as 'Kirkconnel Lea' and 'Fair Helen of Kirconnel'.

Edom o' Gordon

It fell about the Martinmas,
When the wind blew shrill and cold,
Said Edom o' Gordon tae his men,
'We maun draw tae a hold.

'And what a hold sall we draw tae,
My merry men and me?
We will gae tae the house o' the Rodes,
Tae see that fair lady.'

The lady stood on the castle wa'
Beheld both dale and down;
Then she was 'ware o' a host o' men
Cam riding towards the town.

'O see ye not, my merry men a',
O see ye not what I see?
Methinks I see a host o' men;
I marvel wha they be.'

She ween'd it hae been her lovely lord,
As he cam riding hame;
It was the traitor, Edom o' Gordon,
Wha reck'd nae sin nor shame.

She had nae sooner busk'd hersel,
And putten on her gown,
But Edom o' Gordon an' his men
Were round about the town.

Martinmas *11th November*   maun *must*   what a *which*   hold *stronghold, shelter*
ween'd *thought*   reck'd *heeded*   busk'd *dressed*   town *place, settlement*

Edom o' Gordon

They had nae sooner supper set,
    Nae sooner said the grace,
But Edom o' Gordon and his men
    Were light'd about the place.

The lady ran up tae her tower head,
    Sae fast as she could gie,
Tae see if by her fair speeches
    She could wi' him agree.

'Come doun tae me, ye lady gay,
    Come doun, come doun tae me;
This night sall ye lie within mine arms,
    Tomorrow my bride sall be.'

'I winna come doun, ye fals Gordon,
    I winna come doun tae thee;
I winna forsake my ain dear lord,
    That is sae far frae me.'

'Gie owre yer house, ye lady fair,
    Gie owre your house tae me;
Or I sall burn yoursel therein,
    But and your babies three.'

'I winna gie owre, ye fals Gordon,
    Tae nae sic traitor as ye;
And if ye burn my ain dear babes,
    My lord sall may ye dree.

'Now reach my pistol, Claud, my man,
    And charge ye weel my gun;
For, but and I pierce bludey butcher's heart,
    And only graz'd his knee.

light'd *off their horses*   owre *over*   sic *such*   dree *suffer*

Edom o' Gordon

'Set fire to the house!' quo' fals Gordon,
   All wuid wi' dule and ire;
'Fals lady, ye sall rue this deed
   As ye burn in the fire!'

'Wae worth, wae worth ye, Jock, my man!
   I paid ye weel your fee;
Why pu' ye out the gund-wa' stane,
   Lets in the reek tae me?

'And e'en wae worth ye, Jock, my man!
   I paid ye weel your hire;
But now I'm Edom o' Gordon's man,
   Maun either do or die.'

O then bespake her little son,
   Sat on the nurse's knee:
Say, 'Mither dear, gie owre his house,
   For the reek, it smithers me.'

'I wad gie a' my gowd, my bairn,
   Sae wad I a' my fee,
For ae blast o' the western wind,
   To blaw the reek frae thee.'

O then bespake her dochter dear;
   She was baith jimp an' sma':
'O row me in a pair o' sheets,
   And tow me owre the wa'!'

They row'd her in a pair o' sheets,
   And tow'd her owre the wa';
But on the point o' Gordon's spear
   She gat a deadly fa'.

wuid *mad*   dule *grief*   gund-wa' stane *stone closing a garderobe chute*
maun *must*   dochter *daughter*   jimp *slender, trim*   row'd *wrapped*   tow'd *lower*

Edom o' Gordon

O bonnie, bonnie was her mouth,
    And cherry were her cheeks,
And clear, clear was her yellow hair,
    Whereon the red blude drips.

Then wi' his spear he turn'd her owre;
    O gin her face was wane!
He said, 'Ye are the first that ever,
    I wish'd alive again.'

He turn'd her owre and owre again;
    O gin her skin was white!
'I might hae spared thy life
    Tae been some man's delight.'

'Busk and boon, my merry men a',
    For ill dooms I do guess,
I canna look in that bonny face
    As it lies on the grass.'

'Wha looks to freits, my master dear,
    It's freits will follow them;
Let ne'er be said that Edom o' Gordon
    Was daunted by a dame.'

But when the lady saw the fire
    Come flaming owre her head,
She wept and kiss'd her children twain,
    Say, 'Bairns, we been but dead.'

The Gordon then his bugle blew
    And said, 'Awa', awa'!
This house o' the Rodes is a' in flame;
    I haud it time tae gae.'

gin *how*   busk and boon *make ready*   freits *frights (ill omens)*

Edom o' Gordon

And this way look'd her ain dear lord,
As he cam owre the lea;
He saw his castle a' in a lowe,
As far as he could see.

Then sair, o sair, his mind misgave,
And all his heart was wae:
'Put on, put on, my wighty men,
Sae fast as ye can gae.

'Put on, put on, my wighty men,
Sae fast as ye can drie!
For he's that hindmost o' the thrang
Sall ne'er get good o' me.'

Then some they rade, and some they ran,
Out owre the grass and bent;
But ere the foremost could win up,
Both lady and babes were burnt.

And after the Gordon he is gane,
Sae fast as he might drie;
And soon in the Gordon's foul heart's blude
He's wrocken his dear lady.

lowe *fire*   put on *press on*   wighty *valiant*   drie *manage*   wrocken *avenged*
lady is pronounced 'laydee'

NOTES
Adam Gordon of Auchindoun (the Edom o' Gordon of the title; sometimes spelt as Edam) and his men seek shelter in the midst of winter in the House of Rodes. At first the lady of the castle thinks it is her husband returning home but when she realises it is Gordon she does not want to let him in. Her worries are confirmed when he tells her he not only wants shelter but also to share her bed. Getting a pistol, she tries to kill Gordon but only manages to graze his knee. In revenge, and aided by one of the lady's own men, Gordon sets fire to the castle.

Edom o' Gordon

The lady's comely daughter is lowered from the castle wrapped in sheets, but Gordon stabs her with his spear, not realising who it is. He professes that he is sorry for what he has done but the building is now well alight and the lady and her other two children are burnt to death. Gordon and his men ride away just as the lord of the castle and his party approach. Seeing what has been done, the lord pursues Gordon and slays him and many of his men in revenge.

The ballad is reputedly based on the torching of Towie Castle in 1571 by Adam Gordon of Auchindoun. Towie Castle was held by the Forbes family, bitter enemies of the Gordons, and the lady in question is believed to have been Margaret Campbell, the wife of the Master of Forbes. The story goes that she and her children and servants, some twenty-seven souls in all, were suffocated or burned alive. Gordon seems to have escaped unscathed from the atrocity, however. Towie Castle, which lay near the River Don not far from Kildrummy in Aberdeenshire, was rebuilt after the fire but has since been demolished and there are no remains

Other locations for the ballad have been suggested, including Corgarff Castle. This was also a property of the Forbes family and was burned several times before being used as a base against illicit whisky distilling. The castle lies ten miles west of Ballater in a rugged area of Aberdeenshire and can be visited. In the ballad recounted in this book the site is given as the House of Rodes, a property near Duns in Berwickshire in the Borders, although why it has been translated here is not clear as there appears to be no record of such an event.

The ballad, which has several versions, is from Child No 178, and is on record from the middle of the eighteenth century. Another version of the story has the lord avenging himself on Gordon and then throwing himself into the flames of his still burning castle.

Corgarff Castle

The Dowie Houms o' Yarrow

Late at een, drinking the wine,
And ere they paid the lawin',
They set a combat them between,
To fight it in the dawin'.

'O stay at hame, my noble lord!
O stay at hame, my marrow!
My cruel brother will you betray,
On the dowie houms o' Yarrow.'

'O fare ye weel, my lady gay!
O fare ye weel, my Sarah!
For I maun gae, tho' I ne'er return,
Frae the dowie banks o' Yarrow.'

She kiss'd his cheek, she kaim'd his hair,
As she hae done before, O;
She belted on his noble brand,
And he's awa' tae Yarrow.

O he's gane up yon high, high hill;
I wat he gaed wi' sorrow;
And in a den spied nine arm'd men,
In the dowie houms o' Yarrow.

'O are ye come tae drink the wine,
As ye hae done before, O?
Or are you come tae wield the brand,
On the dowie houms o' Yarrow?'

dowie *doleful* houms *flat area beside a river* lawin' *owing (bill)* dawin' *dawn*
marrow *mate (love)* maun *must* kaim'd *combed* brand *sword*

The Dowie Houms o' Yarrow

'I am nae come tae drink the wine,
As I hae done before, O,
But I am come tae wield the brand,
On the dowie houms o' Yarrow.'

Four he hurt and five he slew,
On the dowie houms of Yarrow,
Till that stubborn knight came him behind,
And ran his body though, O.

'Gae hame, gae hame, good brother John,
And tell your sister Sarah
To came and lift her gentle lord,
Who's sleeping sound on Yarrow.'

'Yestreen I dream'd a dolefu' dream;
I ken'd there wad be sorrow;
I dreamed a pu'd the heather green,
On the dowie banks o' Yarrow.'

She gaed up yon high, high hill;
I wat she gaed wi' sorrow;
And in a den spied nine dead men,
On the dowie houms o' Yarrow.

She kiss'd his cheek, she kaim'd his hair,
As she hae done before, O;
She drank the red blude frae him ran,
On the dowie houms o' Yarrow.

'O haud your tongue, my dochter dear,
For what needs a' this sorrow?
I'll wed ye on a better lord
Than him ye lost on Yarrow.'

yestreen *yesterday evening*   pu'd *pulled out*   haud *hold*
dochter *daughter*

The Dowie Houms o' Yarrow

'O haud your tongue, my father dear,
And dinnae grieve your Sarah;
A better lord was never born
Than him I lost on Yarrow.

'Tak hame your ousen, tak home your kye,
For they hae bred our sorrow;
I wiss that they had a' gane mad
When first they cam tae Yarrow.'

dinnae *don't* ousen *oxen* kye *cattle*

Notes

Late at night, after drink has been taken, an unnamed lord (the husband of Sarah) and his brother-in-law (John), decide to fight each other, come the next morning. Sarah begs her lord not to go, but he says he must and he climbs a hill and finds that the lady's brother has, rather unsportingly, brought eight men with him. They fight and the lord wounds or kills several of the men until he himself is run through from behind and slain by brother John. Sarah says she had a premonition that things would go badly and goes and retrieves her lord's corpse. Her father tell her not to grieve as he can find her a better husband, but Sarah says no better man was ever born.

There are several versions of this ballad, when the lady's lord or betrothed is slain by her brother and his men. Similar ballads are 'The Dowie Dens o' Yarrow' and 'The Douglas Tragedy' (as well as other versions), which are all set by the Yarrow Water in the Borders. In the former the lady takes to her bed and dies of a broken heart after her lord is slain, in the latter both the lovers die. Yarrow Water runs from St Mary's Loch in the Borders, eastward until it joins the Ettrick Water at Philiphaugh near Selkirk, eventually flowing into the River Tweed.

The ballad may have originated, according to Sir Walter Scott, from a fight among branches of the Scott family. Walter Scott of Thirlestane got into an argument his brother-in-law, John Scott of Tushielaw, in 1609, and the outcome was Walter's death, probably in a duel.

These branches of the Scotts certainly feuded, although Thirlestane and Tushielaw are located about one and a half miles apart on the north side of the Ettrick Water, not the Yarrow Water, some fourteen or so miles south-west of Selkirk. Traditionally, however, the fight was to the west of Yarrow Kirk and was over the lady's dowry being too generous, hence the last verse 'take home you oxen, take home your kye, it was them that caused this trouble'.

In 1616, however, Walter Scott of Tushielaw effectively eloped with Grizell Scott of Thirlestane, and Walter was then horribly slaughtered by men acting for the Scotts of Thirlestane, so this may be the origin of the story.

Some have suggested that the lady was Mary or Marion Scott of Dryhope, a lovely lass known as the 'Flower of Yarrow'. If it was Mary, however, she did go on to find another lord – if not necessarily a better one – and in 1576 married Walter Scott of Harden, known as 'Old Wat', and one of those that rescued Kinmont Willie Armstrong from Carlisle Castle. Of course, in 'the Dowie Houms of Yarrow', the lady's name is Sarah, and not Mary or Marion, but – of course – Sarah rhymes much better with Yarrow. Dryhope is, at least, in the correct location, located at the eastern end of St Mary's Loch, north of the Yarrow Water.

'The Douglas Tragedy', which is yet a different version, is said to have happened around Blackhouse Tower, long a property of the Douglases, which lies a couple of miles north of the Yarrow – and a couple of miles from Dryhope.

There were towers at Tushielaw, Thirlestane, Dryhope and Blackhouse, but all four are now ruinous and only Dryhope survives to any degree.

The ballad is from Child 214 and, as stated earlier, there are many versions.

The Daemon Lover

'O whaur hae you been, my long, long love,
 This lang seven years and mair?'—
'O I'm come tae seek my former vows,
 Ye granted me before.'

'O hold your tongue o' your former vows,
 For they will breed sad strife;
O hold your tongue o' your former vows,
 For I am become a wife.'

He turned him right and round about,
 And the tears blinded his e'e:
'I wad ne'er trodden on Irish ground,
 If it hadnae been for thee.'

'I might hae had a king's dochter,
 Far, far beyond the sea;
I might hae had a king's dochter,
 Had it nae been for love o' thee.'

'If ye might hae had a king's dochter,
 Yersel' ye have tae blame;
Ye might have ta'en the king's dochter,
 For ye ken'd that I was nane.

'If I wad tae leave my husband dear,
 And my twa bairns also,
O what hae ye tae take me tae,
 If with ye I should gae?'

e'e *eyes* dochter *daughter* ken'd *knew* bairns *children*

75

The Daemon Lover

'I hae seven ships upon the sea —
The eighth brocht me tae land —
With four and twenty bold mariners,
And music on every hand.'

She hae taken up her twa little babes,
Kiss'd them baith cheek and chin:
'O fair ye weel, my ain twa babes,
For I'll ne'er see ye again.'

She set her foot upon the ship,
Nae mariners could she behold;
But the sails were o' the taffetie,
And the mast o' beaten gold.

She hadnae sail'd a league,
A league but barely three,
When dismal grew his countenance,
And drumlie grew his e'e.

They hadnae sail'd a league,
A league but barely three,
Until she espied his cloven foot,
And she wept bitterlie.

'O hold your tongue o' weeping,' says he,
'O' your weeping now let me be;
I will show you how the lillies grow
On the banks o' Italy.'

'O what hills are yon, yon pleasant hills,
That the sun shines sweetly on?'—
'O yon are the hills o' heaven,' he said,
'Whaur you will ne'er win.'

brocht *brought* drumlie *grim* yon *that* win *reach, arrive*

The Daemon Lover

'O whaten mountain is yon,' she said,
'All so dreary wi' frost and snow?'—
'O yon is the mountain o' hell,' he cried,
'Whaur you and I will go!'

He struck the top-mast wi' his hand,
The foremast wi' his knee,
And he brak that gallant ship in twain,
And sank her in the sea.

NOTES

A lady is reunited with a former lover; he wants to renew their acquaintance but during his absence the lady has married and had children and at first she refuses him. He is devastated, but she then asks him where he would take her should she abandon her husband and children. He tells her he has a fleet of fine ships and she goes off with him. Once the journey has begun, however, she notices a change in his demeanour and then she spies that he has a cloven foot and she begins to weep. She then asks what are the sunlit hills she can see and he tells her that is heaven and she will never get there; then she asks about the snow-covered mountain and he informs her that is hell and where she is bound. He then breaks the ship in two, sinking it and drowning the lady.

This ballad is from No Child 243 and was published in 1812.

Binnorie

There were twa sisters sat in a bower;
Binnorie, O Binnorie!
There cam a knight tae be the wooer,
By the bonnie milldams o' Binnorie.

He courted the eldest wi' glove and ring,
But he lov'd the youngest above a' thing.

He courted the eldest wi' brooch and knife,
But lov'd the youngest as his life.

The eldest she was vex'd sair,
And sair envi'd her sister fair.

Intae her bower she could nae rest,
Wi' grief and spite she almost brast.

Upon a mornin' fair and clear,
She cried upon her sister dear:

'O sister, sister, take my hand,
And we'll see oor father's ships tae land.'

She's ta'en her by the milk-white hand,
And led her doun tae the river-strand.

The youngest stood upon a stane,
The eldest cam and threw her in.

brast *burst*   cried upon *called (for help)*

Binnorie

She took her by the middle sma'
And dash'd her bonny back tae the jaw.

'O sister, sister, take my hand!
And I'll make you heir tae a' my land.'

'O sister, sister, tak my middle,
And you'se get my gowd and my gowden girdle.

'O sister, sister, save my life,
And I swear I'll ne'er be nae man's wife.'

'Foul fa' the hand that I should take;
It twin'd me o' my world's mate.

'Your cherry cheeks and yellow hair,
Gars me gae maiden for evermair.'

Sometime she sank, sometimes she swam,
Until she cam doun yon bonny mill-dam.

Out then cam the miller's son,
And saw the fair maid swimming in.

'O father, father, draw your dam!
There's either a mermaid or a milk-white swan.'

The miller hast'd and drew his dam,
And there he found a drown'd woman.

You couldna see her yellow hair,
For the strings o' pearls twisted there.

jaw *wave of water*   twin'd *robbed, deprived*
my worldis mate *my only mate (love) in the world*   gars *makes*   draw *drain*

Binnorie

You couldna see her middle sma',
For gowden girdle that was sae braw.

You couldna see her fingers white,
For gowden rings that was sae grite.

And by there came a harper fine,
That harp'd tae the king at dine.

And when he look'd that lady on,
He sigh'd and made a heavy moan.

He's made a harp o' her breast-bane,
Whose sound wad melt a heart o' stane.

He's ta'en three locks o' her yellow hair,
And wi' them strung his harp sae rare.

He went intae her father's ha',
And there was the court assembled a'.

He laid his harp upon a stane,
And straight it began tae play alane:

'O yonder sits my father, the king,
And yonder sits my mother, the queen;

'And yonder stands by brother, Hugh,
And by him my love, sweet and true.'

But the last tune that the harp play'd then—
Was: 'Wae to my sister, false Ellen!'

grite *great*   dine *dinner*   wae *woe*

Binnorie

Two sisters are courted by the same man, and, although the older sister is the more eligible, he falls in love with the younger sister. The older sister is violently jealous and lures her sister to a river where she pushes her into the water. The younger daughter drowns and her body is found by a miller and his son, and then seen by a passing minstrel. Using her hair (and her breast bone), he fashions a harp, which plays by itself. When he takes back to the sister's home, the harp greets the father, mother, brother and lover on good terms – but then damns her sister, the false Ellen.

This ballad is also known as 'The Twa Sisters'. In that version no mention is made of the breast bone being used for the harp; indeed, it does seem unlikely that a harper would either have the opportunity or the desire to make a harp from a murdered corpse's breast bone. There are many versions of the ballad found in Britain, and many other ballads from northern Europe with the same theme and motifs. The mention of the sister's middle sma' (small waist) is a reference to the fact that she is not pregnant or has had a child, hence she is chaste (or lucky…).

The place Binnorie has not been identified. In 'The Twa Sisters', Binnorie is replaced with Edinburgh, Stirling and St Johns Town (Perth) on the Tay:

> There was twa sisters in a bower,
> *Edinburgh, Edinburgh*
> There was twa sisters in a bower,
> *Stirling for ay.*
> There was twa sisters in a bower,
> There cam a knight tae be their wooer.
> *Bonny St Johnstown stands upon the Tay.*

The ballad is from Child No 10.

The Bonnie Earl o' Moray

Ye Highland and ye Lowlands,
O whaur hae ye been?
They hae slain the Earl o' Moray,
And hae laid him on the green.

'Now wae to be thee, Huntly!
And whairfore did ye sae!
I bade ye bring him wi' ye,
But forbade you him tae slay.

'He was a braw gallant,
And he rid at the ring;
And the bonny Earl o' Moray
O he might hae been a king!

'He was a braw gallant,
And he play'd at the ba';
And the bonny Earl o' Moray
Was the flower amang them a'!

'He was a braw gallant,
And he play'd at the glove;
And the bonny Earl o' Moray,
O he was the queen's love!

O lang will his lady
Look owre the Castle Doune,
Ere she see the Earl o' Moray
Cam sounding through the toun!'

rid at the ring *rode in jousting*   sounding *riding with trumpets blaring*

The Bonnie Earl o' Moray

NOTES

The Earl o' Moray has been slain by men under the orders of the Earl of Huntly, who had been told by the king to seize Moray but not to kill him. The Earl o' Moray is then praised for his attributes in jousting and sports and good breeding and manners, suggesting he was beloved of the queen or could even have himself been the king. Finally, the wife of the Earl o' Moray will miss her husband.

The ballad is based on the slaying of James Stewart, second Stewart Earl of Moray, in February 1592. Moray had been accused of plotting against James VI at Holyrood Palace in Edinburgh, along with Francis Stewart, the mercurial and perhaps dangerous Earl of Bothwell. Some have also suggested that Moray was also showing too much interest in Anne of Denmark, James VI's young wife.

George Gordon, sixth Earl of Huntly and sworn enemy of Moray, was given a commission to hunt down Bothwell and his accomplices, who included the Earl of Moray, and he tracked Moray to the castle at Donibristle on the north shore of the Forth. Apparently being refused entry and one of his men actually being shot, Huntly besieged Moray and set fire to the building and Moray fled along the beach in the dark. It is said that the plume of Moray's helmet had caught fire and it was this that betrayed him. Here he was cornered by Gordon of Gight and others and was summarily slain, having been both shot and stabbed, Gordon slashing him across the face and receiving the cutting remark in return, 'You have spoilt a better face than your own'. Some believed, however, that Moray had been waylaid while asleep and was actually murdered in his bed.

Many were appalled by this act, not least Moray's mother, Margaret Campbell, who had a painting made of her son's dead body, showing all the various wounds. The portrait is preserved at Darnaway Castle, near Forres in Moray, which is the seat of the Earls of Moray. Huntly suffered no punishment and it seems possible that James VI had been party to the murder. The dispute between Moray and Huntly may also have been, at least partly, over possession of the Earldom of Moray (Moray had gained the title through marriage to the heiress Elizabeth Stewart), which Huntly desired for himself, but – whatever the truth of it – Huntly was pardoned and promoted to Marquis.

Donibristle Castle, and the mansion that replaced it, have both been demolished apart from service wings, and stood one and a half miles east of Inverkeithing in Fife. Some stories have the ghostly apparition of Moray still being seen occasionally on the beach, his head ablaze. The Castle Doune mentioned is the impressive Doune Castle, stronghold of the Earls of Albany and then of Moray, near Stirling; this stronghold is open to the public and can be visited.

The ballad is from Child No 181 and was published in 1733.

Glossary

Scots	English	Pronounced
a'	all	aw
aboon	above	aboon
ae	a	aye
ain	own	ain
a' kin	every	a kin
alace	alas	aliss
alane	alone	alane
amang	among	amang
amblit	rode	amblit
and	and	an
ane	one	ane
ance	once	ance
auld	old	all-d
ay	always	aye
aye	yes	eye
ba'ed	waited	baed
bairn	child	bairn
bane	bone	bane
behint	behind	be-hint
biek	bake	beak
biggin	building	biggin
biggit	built	biggit
billie	brother	billy
birk	birch	birk
blaw	blow	blaw
blink	sparkle	blink
blude	blood	blude
blyth	joyous, cheerful	blyth
bodkin	long, sharp pin	bodkin
bonny	beautiful	bonny
bore	hole	bore
bow	bend	bow
bower	lady's chamber in a castle/leafy shelter in a wood or garden	bower
bowt	bolt	bowt
brak	broke	brack
brake	thicket	brake
brand	sword	brand
brast	burst	brast

braw	fine, splendid, brave	braw
brie	brow	bree
brigg	bridge	brigg
brocht	brought	brocht
burd	bird	burd
busk	(to) dress	busk
busk and boon	make ready	busk an boon
but and	and also	but an
ca'	call	caw
cam	came	cam
canna	cannot	canna
chamer	chamber	chaymmer
chap	knock	chap
cled	clad	cled
corbie	crow	corbay
coost	cast	coost
cried upon	called (for help)	cried upon
die	die	dee
deid	dead	deed
dine	dinner	dine
dinnae	don't	dinnay
dochter	daughter	dochter
dolefu'	doleful	dolefu
doun	down	doon
dowie	doleful, sorrowful	dowie
draw	drain	draw
draw up	take up	draw up
dree	suffer	dree
drumlie	grim	drumlie
dule	grief	dule
durst	dare	durst
durstna	dare not	durstna
e'en	eyes	een
een	evening	een
e'e	eyes	ee
e'er	ever	err
eldern	old	eldern
evermair	evermore	evermare
fadge	round thick loaf / dumpy person	faj
faem	foam	fay-em
fail dyke	turf wall	fail dyke
fain	must, obliged to	fain
fain	desirous, eager	fain
fause	false	fawse

fat	well fed, fat	fat
fecht	fight	fecht
fee	wealth, payment	fee
forlorn	lost	forlorn
fornent	in front of	fornent
flatter'd	floated	flatterit
frae	from	fray
freights	frights (ill omens)	freets
friends	relatives	friends
gae	go	gay
gaed	went	gayd
gaen	going	gay-in
gaire	part of garment by knee	gayre
gane	will suffice	gane
gane, gang	gone	gane
gangin'	going, working	gangin
gar	make (happen)	gar
gat	got	gat
gear	property	gear
gie	give	gee
gien	given	gee-in
gilt	gold	gilt
gin	if, whether	gin
gin	how	gin
glamour	spell	glamoor
gleed	fire	gleed
gowd	gold	gowd
gowden	golden	gowdin
greet	cry, wail	greet
greetin'	crying, wailing	greetin
grite	great	grite
guid	good	guid
guid rede gae tae me	give me good advice	guid read gay tay me
gund-wa' stane	stone closing a garderobe chute	gund-wa stane
gurly	stormy, growly	gurly
ha'	hall	haw
hadna(e)	had not	had-na(y)
hae	have	hay
haes	has	hays
half-fou	bushel	half fou
hame	home	hame
happ'd	covered	happt
haud	hold	hod

haugh	water mead	hauch
hause-bane	collar bone	hawz-bane
hold	stronghold, shelter	hold
holland	linen	holland
hooly	gently	hooly
hoose	house	hooss
houm	flat area beside a river, brae	hoom
hoys'd	hoisted	hoyzet
ilk	each	ilk
ilka	every	ilka
Ingland	England	ingland
Inglis	English	inglis
intae	into	intay
jimp	slender, trim	jimp
kaim	comb	kame
ken	know	ken
kept	defended	kept
kinnen	rabbit	kinnen
lady	lady	laydee
laigh	low	laich
laith	loathe	laith
lamer	amber	lammer
lang	long	lang
langer	longer	langer
lap	sprang, leapt	lap
lawfu'	lawful	lawfoo
lawin'	owing, bill	lawin
leavins	leftovers	leavins
lie	lie	lee
lift	sky	lift
light	get down (from a horse), alight	light
mair	more	mare
mak	make	mack
maks mane	laments, grives for	macks mane
making my mane	moaning, lamenting grieving	macking my mane
malison	curse	malison
marrow	mate, partner, love	marrow
Martinmas	11th of November	Martinmass
marvelit	shocked, amazed	marvelit
main	force	main
maun	must	mawn
mavis	song-thrush	mavis

meet	well-fitting	meet
mickle	much, a large amount	mickle
meikle	much, a large amount	meekle
mither	mother	mither
mony	many	mony
mool	earth, mould	mool
movit	take off	moovit
muckle	much, a large amount	muckle
mysel(l)	myself	mysell
my worldis mate	my world's mate (one true love)	my worldis mate
nae	no	nay
nane	none	nane
naebody	nobody	naybuddy
ne'er	never	ne-ir
neisten	next	neestin
nicher	neigh	nicher
norland	north	norland
o'	of	o
ony	any	onay
oor	our	oor
out	out	oot
oot o' hand	immediately	oot o hand
or	ere, before	or
owre	over	o-er
pap	(woman's) breast	pap
pest	plague	pest
poin'd	confiscated, impounded	point
pu'	pull (as in fruit from a tree), pick	poo
put doun	killed, executed	put doon
quire	choir (part of a church)	choir
rade	ride	rad
rashes	rushes	rashes
reck	heed	reck
rede	advice, advise	read
rin	run	rin
roan	variegated colour	roan
row	wrap, roll	row
sae	so	say
sair	sore	sayr
sall	shall	sall
saut	salt	sawt
scale	drive way, get rid of	skale

shoon	shoes	shoon
shot-window	hinged window	shot window
sic	such	sic
siller	silver	siller
sin	sun	sin
skeely	skilful	skeely
skinkl'd	sparkled	skinklt
slae	sloe	slae
sma'	small	smaw
spake	spoke	spake
spare	gap in a dress	spare
speir	ask, inquire, request	spear
stane	stone	stain
strang	strong	strang
syne	next, directly after	sign
tae	to	tay
ta'en	taken	tayin
tane	one	tane
ta'en	taken	tain
targat	shield-shaped ornament	targat
thee	you	thee
theek(it)	thatch(ed)	theek(it)
thou	you	thou
threw	intertwined	threw
tift	breeze, gust of wind	tift
tither	other	tither
toun/town	town, place, settlement	toun
tow	lower (by rope)	tow
tree	spear	tree
twa	two	twa
twas	it was	twaz
twin	rob, deprive	twin
twine	coarse linen	twine
unkind	excessively harsh	unkind
untae	unto	untay
wa'	wall	waw
wad	would	wad
wae	woe, sad	way
wadna(e)	would not	wad-na(y)
wame	womb	wame
wap	bind, splice	wap
wax	grow	wax
wax'd	grew	waxt

Glossary

wearie	sick, weak, weary	weary
ween	think, surmise	ween
weddeen	wedding	weddeen
weel	well	weel
weel-faired	good-looking	weel faired
wha	who	wha
wha is aught	whose	wha is ot
what a	which	what a
whaur	where	wharr
white monie	silver	white mony
win	reach, arrive	win
winna(e)	will not	winna(y)
wiss	wish	wiss
wist	knew, have knowledge of	wist
wot	knew, have knowledge of	wat
wuid	insane, mad	wood
wuid wrath	insane with rage	wood wrath
yae tift	any breeze of wind	yay tift
ye	you	yee
ye'se	you can, you will	yeez
yestreen	yesterday evening, last night	yes-treene
yon	that, those over there	yawn
yoursel(l)	yourself	yoursell

SOME NOTES ON PRONUNCIATION

- 'die' (as in decease) is pronounced 'dee', similarly 'lie' as 'lee'
- 'out' is often pronounced 'oot'
- the 'r' is rolled a little, as 'rr'
- 'and' is pronounced 'an'
- 'ing' at the end of a word is pronounced with the 'g' softly as 'lawin' (for lawing) or 'drawin' (for drawing)
- when words have an 'ie' at the end, such as 'decentlie' instead of 'decently' or 'wearie' instead of 'weary', the last syllable is extended (ie 'decentl□y-ee' or 'weary-e'); similarly 'lady' is often 'laydee'
- when verbs such as 'hunted', 'steered' or 'banished' have a missing 'e', such as 'hunt'd', 'steer'd' or 'banish'd', this changes the sound almost to a 't' (ie 'hunt't' or 'huntit', 'steert' or 'steerit' or 'banisht' or 'banishit')